Growing in Christ

Growing in Christ

becoming

Edited by
Ray E. Barnwell, Sr.

WESLEYAN
PUBLISHING HOUSE
Indianapolis, Indiana

Copyright © 2002 by The Wesleyan Church
Published by Wesleyan Publishing House
Indianapolis, Indiana 46250
Printed in the United States of America
ISBN 0-89827-248-3

Contributing Writers and Editors

Ray E. Barnwell, Sr.
Bob Black
Don Bray
Patricia David
Lee M. Haines
Ron McClung
Blair Ritchey
Darlene Teague
David L. Thompson
Lawrence W. Wilson

Discipleship Project Committee

Earle L. Wilson, Chairman
Ray E. Barnwell Sr., Project Director
Martha Blackburn
Dan Berry
Donald D. Cady
Ross DeMerchant
Steve DeNeff
James Dunn
Russ Gunsalus
Ron McClung
Robert Brown, Advisory Member
Darlene Teague, Advisory Member

Table of Contents

Preface

All living things grow: plants, trees, animals, people, and yes, even your faith in Christ. As a believer, your faith must be growing continually. Growth and development are essential for your spiritual health. The opposite of growth is decay, which leads to death. That is not a pleasant prospect, but it can become a reality for anyone who doesn't take spiritual growth seriously.

Your spiritual growth is important—and not just to you. Your pastor, Sunday School teacher or small group leader, and Christian relatives and friends are all vitally interested in seeing you reach spiritual maturity. In fact, your Heavenly Father takes a direct interest in your spiritual condition! Growing as a believer was not meant to be a solo adventure. It's a journey we take together, a journey called *discipleship*.

And that's where the *Building Faith* series comes in. It is a series of books that will help you grow in the faith, and this book, *Growing in Christ: becoming,* is a vital part of that plan for growth.

As you open the pages of this book, you'll gain the insight you need to become more and more like Christ. The goal is that you will become all that God wants you to be—a living representation of Jesus Christ. That won't happen in a day, a week, or even a year, but you will get there. It's a lifelong journey, and you'll make progress every day.

This book is for people just like you. Let it be your personal guide on the discipleship journey. Many great discoveries await you!

Here are a few of the milestones you'll pass as you explore this book.

Chapter one will help you scan the horizon from a new perspective. It's about developing a Christian worldview—it will help you form a uniquely Christian way of looking at life.

Using our resources for God's glory is the focus of chapter two. There you'll discover that faithful use of all God has entrusted to us is part of His plan for our growth.

Discipline. Few of us like that word, but we all need it. Chapter three will explore the how and why of spiritual disciplines—those practices and habits that help us become more like Christ.

The fourth chapter delves into one of the greatest mysteries in Scripture—the Trinity. You will gain a greater understanding of our awesome God and come away inspired to worship and serve Him more.

The snapshot of Christian history in chapter five will whet your appetite for the study of our rich heritage. You'll meet some of the reformers and revivalists who have shaped the church over the centuries.

What you believe really does make a difference in the way you live. You'll see that in chapter six as you discover the core biblical teachings about faith and salvation.

The final chapter will introduce you to two foundational Scriptures—the Ten Commandments and the Sermon on the Mount. There you'll begin to learn how to study the Bible for yourself.

There's a lot to learn, so let's get started on the exciting journey of *Building Faith!*

RAY E. BARNWELL, SR.

Introduction

Welcome to the exciting journey of discipleship! This book—part of the *Building Faith* series—offers a great opportunity for spiritual growth. In fact, the entire series has been developed for just that purpose: to help you grow as a disciple of Jesus Christ. By participating in this study, you will be shaping your life according to God's Word by using spiritual disciplines such as Bible study, prayer, fasting, Scripture memorization, meditation, and journal writing.

The Goal: Building People

Discipleship is the continuing process of spiritual development. It begins at conversion and continues as long as we live—it's a lifelong journey. Our strategy for making disciples is called *Building People*. The *Building People Strategy* is built upon four core values:

- Sharing Love—Evangelism
- Shaping Lives—Discipleship
- Serving Like Christ—Ministering to Society
- Sending Leaders—Mobilization

Here's how it works: having discovered Christ, you will want to grow in your knowledge of Him—shaping your life according to God's Word. As you do, you will discover a personal ministry, a way to use your spiritual gifts to serve others. Then, having been filled with compassion for others, you will be moved to go into the world, fulfilling the Great Commission by evangelizing the lost—thus completing the cycle of discipleship.

The Process: Building Faith

We implement the *Building People Strategy* through a process called *Building Faith. Building Faith* is a *competencies model*, meaning that it's focused on integrating important abilities into every aspect of a believer's life. These core competencies are organized around five categories:

- Biblical Beliefs

- Lifestyle Practices

- Virtues

- Core Values

- Mission

This process aims to form disciples according to the *Great Commandment* and the *Great Commission*.

The method is summarized in the chart that follows. You'll want to bookmark this page and refer to it often.

Building Faith				
Foundational Beliefs	Lifestyle Practices	Personal Virtues	Core Values	Mission
The Trinity	Worship	Joy	Biblical Authority	Discipling Believers
Salvation by Grace	Prayer and Faith	Peace and Grace	Biblical Authority	Evangelizing the Lost
Authority of the Bible	Practicing the Mind of Christ and Discipline	Faithfulness	Biblical Authority	Discipling Believers; Equipping the Church
Personal Relationship with God	Bible Study and Prayer	Self-Control	Christlikeness; Disciple-Making	Discipling Believers
Identity in Christ	Baptism, Lord's Supper	Humility and Grace	Local Church Centered	Discipling Believers
Church/ Family of God	Biblical Community of Faith Beginning in a Christian Home	Love	Local Church Centered; Servant Leadership	Ministering to Society; Discipling Believers
Eternity/Global Evangelism	Lifestyle Evangelism	Love and Obedience	Disciple-Making; Unity in Diversity	Evangelizing the Lost
Stewardship (Including Good Works, Compassion)	Making Christ Lord of Time, Money, Life	Humility, Patience and Goodness	Disciple-Making; Servant Leadership	Equipping the Church; Ministering to Society
Freedom of the Will	Biblical World View	Obedience	Cultural Relevance; Biblical Authority	Discipling Believers; Equipping the Church
Holiness	Godliness, Loving Obedience to God's Revealed Will	Patience, Gentleness, Kindness, Love	Christlikeness; Disciple-Making	Discipling Believers; Ministering to Society

Foundational Truths

Building Faith is based on ten foundational truths, which are key elements for life transformation. These biblical concepts encompass the scope of Christian thinking. Learning these important concepts will help you grow in the faith.

Practices

Every believer must move from theory to practice. That is, he or she must learn to apply biblical truth to life. The practices identified in *Building Faith* will assist you to enact your faith and will become the evidence of the change that's taken place in your life.

Virtues

Virtues are Christlike qualities that emerge in the life of a believer, replacing sinful thoughts and attitudes. These virtues reveal the developing character of a transformed person and attract others to Christ. These virtues are also known as the *fruit of the Spirit.*

Core Values

Biblical truth must be applied in the framework of Christ's body, the church. The core values are the guiding principles by which the church should function. They are our method of operating, describing *how* we do the things we do.

Mission

Ultimately, believers are called to serve. The mission describes what it is that we do for Christ. Each biblical truth finds a practical expression in our work.

Your Involvement: Spiritual Disciplines

These days, many people who are searching for faith have discovered something exciting in Christian worship. The worship service is the point of entry to most churches. Yet as important as worship is, believers need something more in order to grow in the faith. Most of the new believers I speak with still have questions; they're looking for clarification. And they are longing for Christian relationships. Wouldn't it be great if there was a place you could go to make friends and find answers? Wouldn't it be wonderful if you could discover a forum to open your heart, grow in the faith, and find unconditional love?

There is such a place!

Sunday School and other small group discipleship settings provide exactly that kind of environment for building faith. Discipleship moves beyond worship to involve people in building their faith in the context of loving relationships. Just as the New Testament church was built on teaching and preaching (Acts 5:42), so today's church must be built on Bible study. Gaining a thorough knowledge of the Bible is best done by participating in a Sunday School class or Bible study group in addition to attending worship services. Both are important. One without the other can create an imbalance in your spiritual life. Being connected to a family-like unit that's relationship based is a vital component of discipleship.

In most churches, that caring, nurturing unit is called Sunday School. Other churches achieve this interaction through discipleship groups of various kinds. Whatever the name, day, or place of meeting, the fact is that everyone needs a protected environment in which to discover and practice the faith.

If you want to grow and become more effective in the Christian faith, then I urge you to join a Sunday School class or discipleship group.

Along with involvement in a discipleship class or small group, there are some other simple disciplines that have been proven to enhance spiritual formation. You can boost your spiritual growth by using these simple tools.

Bible Reading and Study

The *Building Faith* series is designed to direct you to the Bible at every point in your study. Each chapter begins with one or two important Scripture passages and includes dozens of Bible references to explore. You can enhance your Bible study by using a good Bible translation, written in today's language, such as the New International Version (NIV).

Scripture Memorization

Memorization is a simple way to gain ownership of important Scripture verses. Each of the chapters in this book includes a key verse to memorize. At the end of the book is a Scripture memory tool—perforated flash cards containing the key verse for each chapter. Use them to memorize these verses and you'll gain confidence in your knowledge of Scripture.

Daily Prayer and Reflection

Time alone with God is perhaps the single most important spiritual practice for any disciple. Spend time in prayer and reflection every day.

Personal Spiritual Journal

Journal writing is a way to enhance time spent in prayer and reflection. Recording observations about your life and faith will help you process what you are learning and clarify the spiritual issues in your life. There is a personal spiritual journal page included in each chapter of this book. At the end of each book is an extended journal section that you may use to expand your journal writing. Take this study as your opportunity to begin the practice of journal writing. You'll be glad you did.

Now, let's get started on the exciting journey of *Building Faith!*

Learning to Think Like a Christian

Worldview

I have been crucified with Christ and I no longer live, but Christ lives in me. The life I live in the body, I live by faith in the Son of God, who loved me and gave himself for me.

—Galatians 2:20

 **Bible Basics**

Ephesians 1:17–23

[17]I keep asking that the God of our Lord Jesus Christ, the glorious Father, may give you the Spirit of wisdom and revelation, so that you may know him better. [18]I pray also that the eyes of your heart may be enlightened in order that you may know the hope to which he has called you, the riches of his glorious inheritance in the saints, [19]and his incomparably great power for us who believe. That power is like the working of his mighty strength, [20]which he exerted in Christ when he raised him from the dead and seated him at his right hand in the heavenly realms [21]far above all rule and authority, power and dominion, and every title that can be given, not only in the present age but also in the one to come. [22]And God placed all things under his feet and appointed him to be head over everything, for the church, [23]which is his body, the fullness of him who fills everything in every way.

Connecting God's Word to Life

What does it mean to know God better? In what ways does that affect the way you live?

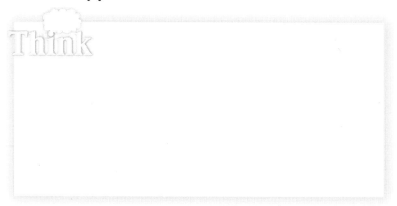

Understanding Worldview

It was a beautiful spring morning in the Grand Canyon. The early light of the sun was illuminating the rock wall that my family and I would climb to get to the top. The only problem was that I couldn't see the trail or even where one might go. I knew there was a way out. In fact the trailhead was only a few feet from where I was standing, but the trail itself seemed to disappear into the mist.

After breaking camp and loading gear on our backs, we started up the trail, over a rise, around a bend, and—there it was—the trail, winding its way up the face of the canyon. My kids know that I have a favorite saying, "What you see depends on where you stand," and it was certainly true that morning in Arizona.

Christians who want to see life clearly need to think about where they stand. They need to identify the intellectual promontory that forms their viewpoint on life, that shapes their thinking, and that becomes the foundation for building their lives. They need to understand their *worldview.*

What Worldview Is

Every human being has a way of thinking that is the conceptual place where they stand. This vantage point from which they look at life is their worldview, the cultural and philosophical perspective that shapes their view of reality. Typically, a person's worldview is absorbed from the influencers around him or her: parents, teachers, church, friends, social and cultural environment, and entertainment. Most of us have never thought to ask the question "What is my worldview?" It's just something we have. It is the platform on which we stand to look at our world. Or, to change the metaphor, it is the lens through which we see what is around us. As a person grows, changes, and learns, his or her worldview can be shaped, restructured, or reinforced by greater insight and understanding.

Dr. Nicholas V. Kroeze has defined worldview as "the product of a person's perception of reality and how that person relates to that reality. The perspective a person has at this level is all-encompassing—embracing history and philosophy, fact and faith, the individual and the cosmos." Charles Colson said that worldview is "nothing less than a framework for understanding all of reality."

> Most of us never ask "What is my worldview?"

An Example of Worldview

Growing up in Chicago, I looked at life differently than my friend Ron, who lived on a farm in central Illinois. As a young teen I visited the farm and ran around with Ron and his friends. I often struggled to understand what they were talking about. His was a world of farming: planting, cultivating, harvesting, caring for animals, morning and evening chores. The rhythms and mystery of nature were frequent subjects of conversation. But none of this applied to me, an inner-city kid. I knew how to travel the streets, take the bus, go downtown on the El. To me, life revolved around sports, especially Cubs games.

In Ron's world, schedules revolved around school activities, which tended to be the social center of the community. In my world, church was all-important. If there was a conflict between school and church, church always had priority. Ron's world was so different than mine that about the only thing we had in common was a love for baseball. Our friendship didn't endure because there was so little common ground.

At the time, neither of us was aware of the difference of our worldviews; we just knew that we didn't always understand where the other was coming from. I had never asked the question, "What is my worldview?" I simply had a way of looking at life that made sense to me and provided a structure for explaining life's circumstances.

Worldview in Action

I was in my middle twenties when my wife, our daughter, and I moved to the interior of Papua New Guinea to live among tribal people. I had never considered how fundamentally different the worldview of an animist only a handful of years removed from the stone age would be from a twentieth-century, urban North American. Of course I realized there would be cultural differences, religious issues, and lifestyle changes, but I did not understand how completely and radically differently we would view life.

My New Guinean friend Wendega and I lived at different ends of the same village geographically, but we lived on different planets in regard to our understanding of reality. Here is a comparison of our two perspectives that may explain the powerful way in which worldviews shape our understanding of life.

Wedenga's World	My World
Pre-scientific: The world is observed and explained with logic not informed by science. I once was told that a fruit "marata" would be ripe when enough mosquitoes had deposited their blood into the plant.	**Scientific:** The laws of science shape my understanding of reality: photosynthesis, gravity, second law of thermodynamics help explain my experience.
Animistic: All of creation has spiritual quality so mountains, trees, rivers, animals along with people are spiritually involved together.	**Theistic:** There is one God, Jehovah, who has created humankind in His own image so that they can commune together. Clear differentiation between humans and rest of creation.
Material: Spiritual blessing is always perceived through material success: gardens grow, animals reproduce, and children are born because the spirits are satisfied.	**Spiritual:** Spiritual blessing comes from God in a variety of ways that may seem strange at first. Sometimes it is in material gain or a better job, but other times illness or difficulty result in new perspectives or direction we see as God's blessing.
Economy Driven: Relationships are driven by economic partnerships. Two clans agree on a bride price that links them economically through the man and woman who marry. Romantic love is not considered. Wendega's language does not have a word similar to ours for love.	**Driven by Love:** Relationships are best driven by love with God and others. Will, emotion, affection come together so that we make a deep personal commitment for the good of others. Romance is central to marriage and good feelings are key to friendships.
Clan Centered: The clan makes decisions and individuals see themselves as part of a group.	**Individualistic:** Decisions are made by the individual, and while peer pressure is real, individuals are responsible for their own decisions.

I soon discovered that when I, as a missionary, invited a New Guinean to make a personal decision for Christ based on God's love for him, there was major misunderstanding between us because our worldviews were so different. In fact, I learned after years of ministry in New Guinea that many of the early "believers" had been instructed by their village leaders to convert so they could learn the secrets of our wealth. As our understanding of worldview issues increased and we were better able to understand the deep felt needs of the people, meaningful teaching of the Scripture became possible, and the power of God's Word changed lives.

Have you encountered anyone with a view of life that is radically different from your own? What was it like?

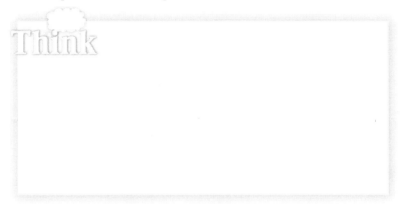

Dangers of a Misguided Worldview

A person's worldview has great power to shape his or her life. We respond to other people socially based on our views of the world, which may be different from theirs. Much misunderstanding and miscommunication happen because we have dissimilar ways of understanding reality.

The Negative Power of Worldview

For example, an African-American woman who has grown to adulthood in an environment that communicates she is inferior, inadequate, and dangerous and has faced the constant pressure of economic insecurity will have a fundamentally different view of reality than will a white, middle-class woman who has never known want and has always encountered her world from a position of power.

I grew up in an economically limited pastor's home but was constantly affirmed with the advice that hard work, education, and discipline would allow me to become whatever God wanted me to be. I looked at life from a position of power, from the vantage point of the cultural majority. And what was true for me, I was taught, was true for black people as well. They were disadvantaged because they simply weren't willing to do what we did. Only much later in life did I begin to understand the power of one's worldview to shape reality and how incredibly hard it is to break free from the confines of a negative worldview and become something different.

Where did you grow up? What were the values that shaped your life? What was the cultural platform that shaped your view of reality?

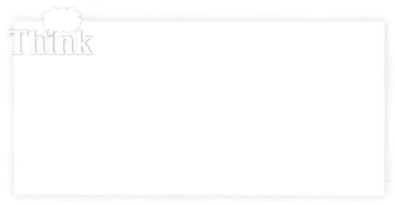

The Limiting Power of Worldview

The principle that worldview shapes and limits a person's reality is seen in some studies done by church growth researchers. Years ago the Fuller Institute of Church Growth discovered that most pastors would only lead a church in growing to the size of the congregation that they themselves grew up in. In other words, the "congregational worldview" that was shaped by the pastors' childhood church experiences created psychological and social boundaries that kept them from expanded ministry. When they led a church to the size of their childhood congregation, internal motivators were satisfied; there was no need to push beyond. Researchers found also that the organizational understanding and social expectations of a congregation were defined by a pastor's worldview, so even the mechanics of leading a church were affected.

If childhood church experiences can shape the professional identity of a minister so powerfully, imagine the effect that worldview will have on the life of a child who happens to grow up in an urban ghetto.

Self-Focused Worldviews

Religious sociologists tell us that many young adults today are not motivated by loyalty to an organization but by the satisfaction of personal needs. For example, rather than identifying with a single congregation, seeing themselves as a vital part of a church family, and investing themselves in its development, some Christians may attend multiple churches in order to satisfy multiple felt needs. By rotating through a variety of congregations, they may enjoy the music of one, the children's ministry of another, the social or sports emphasis of a third, and the community of yet a fourth.

This consumer mentality may help to create a worldview in their children in which instability and self-orientation predominate rather than service, investment, and commitment. This is another example of the power of worldview.

Has your worldview affected your life negatively or positively? How so?

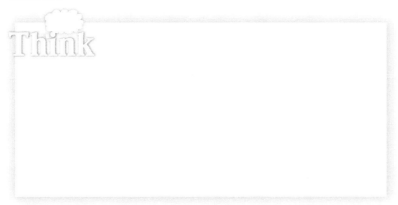

Understanding Your Worldview

Charles Colson, famed both for his role in President Nixon's Watergate scandal and as founder of Prison Fellowship, co-wrote the powerful book *How Now Shall We Live?* to help modern believers develop a biblical worldview. According to Colson, every worldview can be analyzed by the way it answers three basic questions.

- Where did we come from and who are we?

- What has gone wrong with the world?

- What can we do to fix it?

Whether you are aware of it or not, you have probably formed answers to those questions. How did that happen? Where did your worldview come from?

Parental Influence

Worldview begins to develop in infancy as parents pour their perspectives, values, and expectations into their children. A father's complaint that he never has enough money, a mom's encouragement to excellence, family stories of past triumphs or defeats: these are the tools used to construct a worldview.

As a small child, my mind was filled with Bible stories and fairy tales that had moral meaning. It seemed as if I heard the story a thousand times of Abraham Lincoln walking miles to return two pennies he had accidentally overcharged a customer. Our home was filled with biblical sayings like "Pride goes before a fall and a haughty spirit before destruction" and with others that almost sounded biblical but probably weren't, like "After laughter comes tears."

Outside Influences

Influences outside the home affect worldview also. The games children play, the books they read, and the television programs and movies they watch all contribute to the process of forming their worldview. Many television sitcoms use the topics of sex or tension of interpersonal conflict between parents to attract viewers. Certainly this constant diet of a dysfunctional view of relationships can distort a child's expectations for marriage. There is a truism in the world of computers that has application for most of life: "Garbage In, Garbage Out." The influences that we allow into our own lives and those of our children can subtly but powerfully shape our view of reality.

> Secular thinking pervades our culture.

Pervasive Secularism

In spite of our best efforts to control outside influences on our own thinking and that of our children, secular culture is pervasive and powerful. Charles Colson and co-author Nancy Pearcey tell the story of Dave Mulholland and his daughter Katy who go to Epcot in Orlando, Florida, for a father-and-daughter trip. There, the science exhibits powerfully communicated the idea that nature is "all there is or ever was or ever will be," to paraphrase famed astronomer Carl Sagan's litany. To his surprise, Mulholland discovered that his teenage daughter had fully accepted the idea that science can explain all of life and that Christianity is an outmoded and inadequate guide for living.

Fifty years ago the general culture still operated from a theistic bias. Because of his own faith and life example and because his daughter had confessed faith in Christ as a pre-teen, Dave assumed that she had adopted the same worldview that he held. His assumptions about her worldview were devastatingly wrong. Secular thinking pervades our culture through entertainment, the media, and education. It can exert a powerful effect on our own view of the world.

Taking Control of Your Worldview

Understanding your worldview and developing it as a Christian is hard work that takes careful thinking, lots of courage, and a willingness to open your mind to the teaching of Scripture. Just as you accepted Jesus Christ as your Savior by faith, your next step is to allow the Bible to instruct you about God and His world. That requires a two-fold commitment to become a learner, regardless of your age or place in life, and to accept God's Word as the ultimate authority in matters of faith and life.

What are the influences that have shaped your worldview? Would you say that you have a Christian worldview? Why or why not?

Building a Biblical Worldview

Many Christians in North America are trying to understand the Christian faith based upon a secular worldview. That's like trying to find the right road with the wrong map: their own view of the world is contrary to the very truth they seek to understand. No wonder they find Christianity confusing! The good news is that the Bible was written to inform us about God and His world, and one of the key functions of Scripture is to help us see the world as God does.

One of the miracles of the Bible is that it speaks God's truth to every generation, in every culture. I have seen tribal people, barely literate, with limited education, coming from an animistic culture, discover God's purpose for their lives from Scripture. On the other hand, sophisticated, well-educated Europeans steeped in Marxism have recognized God's truth in Scripture also and have allowed their lives to be shaped by it. Even though Anglos and Africans, Europeans and Asians, Latinos and Pacific Islanders will always view the world through their own cultural biases, in Christ we have common ground on core biblical issues.

Biblical Foundations for Worldview

From Genesis to Revelation the Bible reveals a worldview that is unique. Here are a few Scriptures that illustrate the Christian worldview—the way God thinks about the world.

Genesis 1:1. "In the beginning God created the heavens and the earth." The issue is not *how* God created the world but *that* He did. The fact that God is the creator of all that exists is the starting point for understanding the world. It informs our thinking about nature, the value of science, even our own bodies.

> God's love is the central thought in our view of the world.

Genesis 1:26–30. "God said, 'Let us make man in our image, in our likeness, and let them rule over the fish of the sea, and the birds of the air, over the livestock, over all the earth." The Bible makes a distinction between the creation of animals and of human beings, thus placing a different value on people than on other animals. Human beings are given mastery over the planet, including all other created things, with the instruction to use them wisely. This belief shapes our view of the planet and environmental issues, including the so-called animal rights movement.

John 3:16. "For God so loved the world that he gave his one and only Son, that whoever believes in him shall not perish but have eternal life." Typically, people define God based on their own experience of life. God's Word offers a wider view of reality. God loved us before we even knew of His existence. He acted to save us based only on His love for us and not on any good thing we had done. God's love for us is the central thought in our view of the world—and of ourselves.

Matthew 5–7. These three chapters of the Bible are known as Jesus' Sermon on the Mount (a study of this passage is included in Chapter 7 of this book). In this teaching, Jesus defines the way in which God expects us to think and behave, in contrast with the "normal" way that most, even religious, people live. The Christian way of understanding ourselves and our responsibility toward God and other people is radically different from that of popular culture.

Romans 1:18–32. "Although they claimed to be wise, they became fools and exchanged the glory of the immortal God for images made to look like mortal man" (v. 22). Scripture teaches that human beings have foolishly rebelled against God and His plan for the world. There are many social and religious theories which suggest that people are essentially good. The Bible presents a different picture of the human condition—it is flawed by sin. The Apostle Paul restates the effect of sin upon our world several times in the book of Romans (see Rom. 3:23; 6:23; 7:7–25). Could you explain the natural relationship of human beings to God in your own words?

Romans 6:11–12. "In the same way count yourselves dead to sin but alive to God in Christ Jesus. Therefore do not let sin reign in your mortal body so that you obey it evil desires." Just as some people believe that human beings are essentially good, others believe that the grip of sin is so strong that we can never be freed from it. These verses help us see that through the transforming power of Christ a person can be free from the power of sin. We do not need to be slaves to our sinful desires. God can make us free.

Matthew 24:14 (see also Matt. 28:20; Rom. 16:26). "And this gospel of the kingdom will be preached in all the world as a witness to all the nations, and then the end will come." God sees the whole world, and we must also. Global vision is the foundation of every Christian ministry because it reflects the way God things (He ". . . so loved the world") and is part of His strategic plan to bring salvation to all people. Christians have a true worldview in that they have a view of life that encompasses the whole world.

Passage	Observations	Observations about the World
Gen. 1:1		
Gen. 1:26–30		
John 3:16		
Matt. 5–7		
Rom. 1:18–32		
Rom. 6:11–12		
Matt. 24:14 (see also Matt. 28:20; Rom. 16:26		

What new things did you learn about God and the world from these verses?

Biblical Worldview Summarized

Our world today is highly relational and increasingly informal. We greet one another by first names regardless of age or position. The connection of the moment usually seems most important, and this often results in shallow relationships.

It seems that those same values bleed over into our way of relating to God. Our culture desires a first name, shallow relationship with God that makes His resources available to us but does not make us available to Him. The antidote to this is a deeper understanding of who God is. That is called *theology*, the study of God. A Christian worldview is rooted in theology.

There are many ways to articulate a Christian worldview, one that is based on a thorough knowledge of God. Here is one example. It reflects a theology based on Scripture and representing a Wesleyan-Arminian perspective.

- God is the beginning and end of everything. He is the creator of all that exists. He is worthy of our worship and obedience.

- God's creation was perfect, in complete harmony with itself and with Him. God created people in a distinct act and in His own image and gave human beings the ability and authority to make moral decisions and to rule over creation on His behalf.

- Adam, the first person, chose to disobey God and introduced sin into the world. The result was disharmony in the created world and separation between God and people. Adam's act of rebellion changed the very moral nature of human beings, making them self-centered. This rebellion alienated the human race from God and brought everyone and everything under God's judgment.

- God requires that sinful actions be brought to justice. He has declared that the "wages of sin" is death, therefore all must die. But because He loved the world, God sent His Son, Jesus, who is perfect, to die on our behalf. Through faith in Jesus, we may be accepted by God and be at peace with Him.

- Human beings carry the image of God within them in that they are morally responsible for their actions. They have been empowered by God to make moral choices. God has placed their eternal destiny in their own hands. Through Christ, God has made it possible for everyone to be saved by faith; He never violates the right of people to make their own decisions.

> ## Human beings have been empowered by God to make moral choices.

- After Jesus Christ died for our sin, He was raised from the dead in a display of God's power, demonstrating that evil has been completely defeated. This same power is released in this world by the Holy Spirit to redeem people, society, and return wholeness to creation. With the help of the Holy Spirit, believers are able to be free from the self-centeredness with which they were born. They are free from the guilt of past sin, free to live righteously, and able to enjoy unbroken communion with God.

- When believers open their hearts to the power of the Holy Spirit and bring their lives into alignment with the teaching of Scripture, they have great joy and deep personal fulfillment. They will live with integrity, humility, and deep compassion for others, reflecting God's character in their own.

> ## Through Christ, everyone may be saved by faith.

- All believers should love God and their neighbors wholeheartedly. The greatest expression of God's love is that He provided salvation by sending Jesus to earth. The greatest expression of human love is to take the good news of God's redemptive love to others.

Write a brief outline of your view of the world. Is it compatible with Scripture?

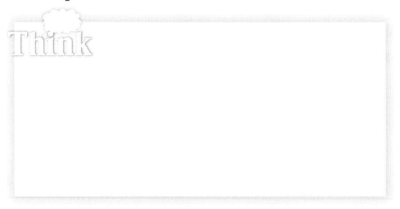

The Benefits of a Christian Worldview

We've seen that a person's worldview can be a negative or limiting factor in his or her life. In the same way, a healthy view of the world can bring great power for living. Christians enjoy a sense of peace and optimism because of the unique way in which they interpret life. Here are some benefits of a Christian worldview.

Hope

My younger sister has been gravely ill for many years. She is a deeply committed believer, and thousands of people have been praying for her healing. But year after year, the death grip of her illness has tightened. Her suffering has become more pronounced, and her pain is almost unbearable. We have asked God to take her to heaven, and even that prayer is yet to be answered.

But because I believe that God is completely loving, I trust Him with my sister's life. I believe that there is a greater purpose at stake that will bring meaning to her suffering. Without this perspective it would be impossible to not be angry, bitter, and disillusioned. But I am not, and neither is her godly husband. Our Christian view of the world brings hope.

Freedom

As Christians, we rejoice that our sins are forgiven and that the Holy Spirit has cleansed our hearts and continues that sanctifying work in practical ways each day. So when we are tempted to sin, we are reminded that we have the ability to say "no." God's Spirit calls us daily to a life of freedom, discipline, and delight in doing good. Where once our minds were captured by negative and destructive forces, now the power of good is released in us. Our view of the world gives us encouragement to follow God wholeheartedly.

Stewardship

We believe that God's redemptive work includes all of creation and that He still calls us to be good managers, or stewards, of earth. Therefore we look for ways to

> Our view of the world gives us encouragement to follow God wholeheartedly.

improve our environment, to conserve the world's natural resources, and to support initiatives that will honor God's values for the earth. All creation groans, the Apostle Paul wrote, waiting for the return of Christ and the full restoration of His perfection (Rom. 8:19). But as we wait for Him, we contribute to God's glory by caring for His world.

Mission

Perhaps the greatest impact that my Christian worldview has had on my life is the formation of my sense of mission. Through the loving example of my parents and the faithful ministry of Sunday School teachers and youth leaders, I gave my heart to Christ as a young person and committed myself to living for Him. Just as these godly adults showed their love for me in Christ, I resolved to love others for Him.

Prompted by this sense of mission, I went door to door while in college, inviting people to church, even though I found it intimidating at first. Later, my wife and I entered parish ministry, and then, to our great surprise, we sensed that God was leading us to so serve as missionaries. We eventually went to the interior of Papua New Guinea to work among tribal people.

Throughout my life, my worldview has focused my attention on the fact that nothing is of greater importance than telling people of God's love. Convinced of this, I chose to align myself with the role God had picked for me. I discovered that God can be relied upon completely, for He is fully faithful. My worldview has formed the sense of purpose for my life.

Lifestyle

A Christian worldview has affected my life in many practical ways. For example, our sense of mission has caused our family to purchase a smaller home and drive used cars so that we might financially support God's work. As I write this, my wife and I are praying about a contribution to our church's building fund, which we will give over and above our tithe to the church and our faith promise for global missions. We do this because we understand that God loved us first and without reservation, and we have the honor of being like Him as we love others.

Jesus said to His disciples in John 20:21, "As the Father has sent me so I am sending you. . . ." If we accept a Christian worldview, we accept the notion that we have been sent by God. So the question each one of us is "Where is God sending me?"

Paul was a new believer who recognized that God was sending him to help the poor, so he leads a group of people each year who remodel homes for the very poor. Patty risked taking a short-term trip to Africa a few years ago, and now she leads a group of people every year in ministering to others in the far parts of the world. Susan uses her bubbly personality and in-home cosmetics business to connect with women and tell them of God's love. Garry and Mary Anne, with their two children, recently sold their business and moved overseas to use their business skills to do the administrative work for a missions agency.

Where is God sending you?

What is your outlook on life? List some ways that a Christian worldview gives you a sense of hope and purpose.

📚 To Learn More

Clean Living in a Dirty World edited by Stephen M. Miller
How Now Shall We Live? by Charles Colson and Nancy Pearcey
What Jesus Said About . . . edited by Everett Leadingham
Who's ~~On~~ First? edited by Everett Leadingham

All additional books and resources are available from Wesleyan Publishing House at www.wesleyan.org/wph or by calling 800.4.WESLEY (800.493.7539).

Personal Spiritual Journal

_____

_____

_____

_____

_____

_____

_____

_____

_____

_____

_____

_____

_____

My Prayer Today—

_____

_____

_____

_____

CHAPTER 2

Living on Borrowed Time

Stewardship

> *His master replied, "Well done, good and faithful servant! You*
> *have been faithful with a few things; I will put you in charge*
> *of many things. Come and share your master's happiness!"*

—Matthew 25:21

 **Bible Basics**

Matthew 25:14–30

[14]"Again, it will be like a man going on a journey, who called his servants and entrusted his property to them. [15]To one he gave five talents of money, to another two talents, and to another one talent, each according to his ability. Then he went on his journey. [16]The man who had received the five talents went at once and put his money to work and gained five more. [17]So also, the one with the two talents gained two more. [18]But the man who had received the one talent went off, dug a hole in the ground and hid his master's money. [19]After a long time the master of those servants returned and settled accounts with them. [20]The man who had received the five talents brought the other five. "Master," he said, "you entrusted me with five talents. See, I have gained five more." [21]His master replied, "Well done, good and faithful servant! You have been faithful with a few things; I will put you in charge of many things. Come and share your master's happiness!" [22]"The man with the two talents also came. "Master," he said, "you entrusted me

with two talents; see, I have gained two more." ²³His master replied, "Well done, good and faithful servant! You have been faithful with a few things; I will put you in charge of many things. Come and share your master's happiness!" ²⁴Then the man who had received the one talent came. "Master," he said, "I knew that you are a hard man, harvesting where you have not sown and gathering where you have not scattered seed. ²⁵So I was afraid and went out and hid your talent in the ground. See, here is what belongs to you." ²⁶His master replied, "You wicked, lazy servant! So you knew that I harvest where I have not sown and gather where I have not scattered seed? ²⁷Well then, you should have put my money on deposit with the bankers, so that when I returned I would have received it back with interest. ²⁸Take the talent from him and give it to the one who has the ten talents. ²⁹For everyone who has will be given more, and he will have an abundance. Whoever does not have, even what he has will be taken from him. ³⁰And throw that worthless servant outside, into the darkness, where there will be weeping and gnashing of teeth."

Connecting God's Word to Life

What are some of the things that God has entrusted to you?

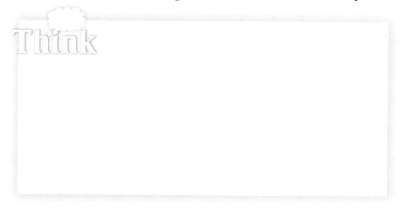

The Meaning of "Stewardship"

Though Jesus didn't use the word *steward* in His parable (Matt. 25:14–30), when the master entrusted money to them, that's what they became. A steward is simply a manager, someone who acts on behalf of another, overseeing employees, resources, and business matters. Stewardship, therefore, is the proper management of everything that God has given to us, including time, talent, and treasure.

In the story, Jesus made it clear that each of us has been given something in trust—some resource or ability that we are to use for His glory.

The Stewardship of Time

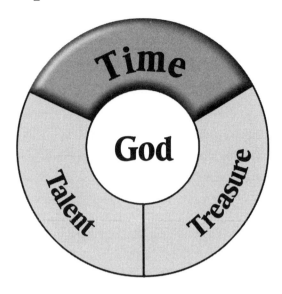

Time is a great equalizer of humanity. While we may not all live the same number of years, each of us has twenty-four hours a day—no more, no less. So time is an extremely valuable commodity which God has entrusted to us.

Benjamin Franklin said, "Dost thou love life, then do not squander time, for that's the stuff life is made of." Paul urged us to take our stewardship of time very seriously. "Therefore be careful how you walk, not as unwise men but as wise, making the most of your time, because the days are evil" (Eph. 5:15–16, NASB). Jesus said, "As long as it is day, we must do the work of him who sent me. Night is coming, when no one can work" (Luke 9:4). The Psalmist prayed, "So teach us to number our days, That we may gain a heart of wisdom" (Ps. 90:12, NKJV). All these passages challenge us to use of our time well.

Valuing Time

An anonymous author has posed this proposition:

> Imagine there is a bank that credits your account each morning with $86,400. It carries over no balance from day to day. Every evening it deletes whatever part of the balance you failed use during the day.
>
> What would you do? Draw out every cent, of course!

Each of us has such a bank. Its name is TIME. Every morning, it credits you with 86,400 seconds. Every night it writes off, as lost, whatever of this you have failed to invest to good purpose. It carries over no balance. It allows no overdraft. Each day it opens a new account for you. Each night it burns the remains of the day. If you fail to use the day's deposits, the loss is yours. There is no going back. There is no drawing against the tomorrow. You must live in the present on today's deposits. Invest it so as to get from it the utmost in health, happiness, and success! The clock is running. Make the most of today.

Planning Time

Have you ever looked at an especially productive person and wondered, "How does he do it? How does he get so much done?"

Probably part of his secret is that he manages his time effectively. Victor Hugo, the philosopher, said, "Where no plan is laid, where the disposal of time is surrendered merely to chance, chaos will soon reign."

> The clock is running. Make the most of today.

One of the simplest ways we can plan our time is to make a *to do* list. Some people work well with a daily list. Others work better with a weekly list. We should use the method that works best for us.

Some things deserve more time. We need to work on some responsibilities when we are at our freshest. They require our full attention. We should plan our time so that we give our best energy to these projects.

Prioritizing Time

Not everything we do is of equal importance. As we write down the things we need to accomplish, we may even wish to assign them a priority value and work on "number one" first, then "number two" second, and so forth, until we work our way through our list.

Fred Smith said, "Since my life is measured by time, I have a responsibility to control it. Most of us don't let other people spend our money; likewise, we should limit their power to spend our time."

Occasionally we hear people say, "I don't have the time." That is very seldom strictly true. We would be more honest if we simply said, "I haven't worked that into my priority list yet" or "I have not found a way to move that higher on my priority list yet." As we learn to prioritize our tasks we will be able to effectively accommodate the reasonable requests of other people.

Someone humorously said, "You cannot overestimate the unimportance of practically everything." While we believe some things are extremely important, things of eternal value, it is easy to get caught up in the trivial, the unimportant.

> As we prioritize our tasks we will be able to accommodate the reasonable requests of other people.

Dr. J. H. Jowett said, "It is never the supremely busy men who have no time. So compact and systematic is the regulation of their day that whenever you make a demand on them, they seem to find additional corners to offer for unselfish service."

So it isn't how much time we have; it's how we use it. It's how we prioritize it in terms of what's important to us.

Remember that what seems unimportant to us may be extremely important to someone else. Charles Francis Adams was a nineteenth-century political figure and diplomat. He kept a diary and one day he entered: "Went fishing with my son today—a day wasted." His son, Brook Adams, also kept a diary. On that same day Brook Adams made this entry: "Went fishing with my father—the most wonderful day of my life!"

> What's important to you? Invest your time in those things.

What's important to you? Are you spending time with God? Time with His Word? Time with family? Time in fellowship with Christian friends? Decide what is important. Decide what has eternal value. Then invest your time in those things.

Dwight Thompson said, "You can spend your life any way you want to, but you can only spend it once." As stewards of the time God has given us, we want to invest it in such a way that we will hear Him say, "Well done, good and faithful servant."

What robs your time? What items could you re-prioritize in order to focus on what's really important?

The Stewardship of Talent

As Christians, each of us has some ability or abilities—Scripture uses the term *gifts*—that God has given us in order to serve others. A spiritual gift is the God-given ability to minister as a part of the body of Christ, either in building up the body, adding to the body, or both. We do not manufacture these gifts. They come from God. As stewards, we are responsible to use them for Him.

Discovering Gifts

The Bible teaches that God has given every believer one or more spiritual gifts. In Eph. 4:11–12, in fact, we learn that God has given some people to the church with specific gifts—apostles, prophets, evangelists, pastors, and teachers—to equip others for Christian service.

Paul wrote, "Now to *each one* the manifestation of the Spirit is given for the common good" (Rom. 12:7, italics added). To discover more about the different types of spiritual gifts, read Eph. 4:7–13, Rom. 12:3–8, and 1 Cor. 12:1–11, 27 31.

> You will discover that God has uniquely gifted you too!

We should not be disappointed if our gifts are different from someone else whom we admire. Paul makes it clear that the Holy Spirit gives different gifts to different people, as He sees best (1 Cor. 12:4, 11). If you are not sure what your spiritual gift is, you will find a spiritual gift inventory helpful in analyzing your strengths and weakness, your desires and passions for ministry.

One way to discover our spiritual gifts is by volunteering for various ministries and looking for ministries that fit your giftedness. Many years before he became president, Abraham Lincoln gathered together a group of men to fight in the Black Hawk War. Because he was the one who gathered the militia together, he held the rank of captain. However, Lincoln knew very little about soldiering. He had difficulty even getting the men to march. One day when they came to a fence, Lincoln could not remember the commands necessary to get them through a gate into another field. So he shouted: "This company is dismissed for two minutes, when it will fall in again on the other side of the gate."

Fortunately, Lincoln discovered what he could do and went on to use his talents and gifts appropriately to become one of our greatest presidents. Don't be discouraged if you try some things that don't work for you. Keep trying and you will discover what God has uniquely gifted you to do. It will be something that honors Him and blesses others.

Using Gifts

These gifts are given so that we may use them, not hide them. Paul advised Timothy not to neglect the gift that had been given to him (1 Tim. 4:14). Just as a gift that is left wrapped under the Christmas tree never brings joy to the person for whom it was intended, so an unused spiritual gift brings no fulfillment to the person who should be using it. Neither does it bring blessing to those who would benefit from its use. Paul urged Timothy to "fan into flame the gift of God" (2 Tim. 1:6). While we cannot manufacture gifts, we can improve our effectiveness through study and experience.

Spiritual gifts are not given to us only for our own enjoyment. Peter insisted that "each one should use whatever gift he has received to serve others" (1 Pet. 4:10–11). Just as the servant in the story of the talents should not have hidden his talent of money, neither should we hide our talents and abilities. God has gifted us in order to be a blessing to other people. We must invest our gifts in such a way that the church is strengthened and advanced.

Distinguishing Gifts and Skills

From a biblical perspective, carpentry is a talent or a skill, not a gift. But a person with the gift of serving might combine the talent or skill of carpentry and be a great blessing in the kingdom of God. The talent of singing is not a biblical gift. Yet the gift of exhortation, or encouragement, may combine with the talent of singing to touch the hearts of many people. As stewards of the talents and gifts God has given us, we should invest them in such a way that we will hear Him say, "Well done, good and faithful servant."

Do you know what your spiritual gifts are? If so, in what ways have you been using them? If not, what steps can you take to determine what your gifts are?

The Stewardship of Treasure

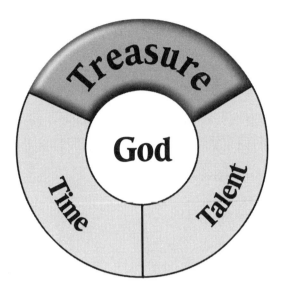

Just as we don't all have the same spiritual gifts, we have different measures of financial resources as well. However, while we don't have equal resources, we can all give our best effort. Each of us is responsible for what we do with the financial resources God has given.

Maturing in Giving

Dr. Ron Kelly observes three levels of giving for Christians.

Level One: What I Ought to Do. In the Old Testament we read about four kings who attacked the cities of Sodom and Gomorrah and carried off the goods and food and even some people, including Abraham's nephew Lot. Abraham rounded up his servants and pursued the kings. After routing the enemy, he returned home with Lot and all the possessions that had been taken. In gratitude, Abraham gave a tithe (10 percent) of all he recovered to a priest named Melchizedek (see Gen. 14:1–20). This was before the law was given and, as far as we know, it was before God gave any instructions about tithing. Yet Abraham felt a desire to give. It's where all of us begin. Since God has given to us, we ought to give to Him.

Level Two: The Tithe Is What I'm Expected to Do. God gave specific instructions through the prophet Malachi for the people to bring "the whole tithe into the storehouse" (Mal. 3:10). This concept is called *storehouse tithing*. In those days, the storehouse was the Temple. In our day, the equivalent is bringing the tithe into one's local church.

God even follows that instruction with a challenging promise: "'Test me in this,' says the LORD Almighty, 'and see if I will not throw open the floodgates of heaven and pour out so much blessing that you will not have room enough for it.'"

Sometimes people say, "Well, that is Old Testament teaching," as if we are no longer bound by it. However, while tithing is commanded in the Old Testament, it is commended in the New Testament. When Jesus confronted the teachers of the law and the Pharisees about their hypocrisy, He observed that they were meticulous about tithing, yet they neglected things like justice, mercy, and faithfulness. He said, "You should have practiced the latter, without neglecting the former" (Matt. 23:23). In other words, while disgusted with their hypocrisy, He encouraged them to continue tithing.

> A grateful heart does not stop with tithing.

Level Three: All I Have Belongs to God and I Am Allowed to Use It. This is what we have been emphasizing throughout this chapter. A grateful heart does not stop with the tithe. The Scripture speaks of "tithes and offerings" (Malachi 3:8). So in addition to the 10 percent, we will give offerings out of the generosity of our hearts.

Developing Positive Attitudes

Two people can drop the same amount of money in the offering plate with quite different motivations. One may give joyfully while the other gives grudgingly. It is easy to discern which one will receive the greater blessing. Let's examine five positive attitudes of a good steward.

We Give Willingly. In Acts 4:34–35, we read about people who even sold property and brought the proceeds to the apostles to distribute to those who were needy. Nobody forced them to do this. They did it willingly.

We Give Cheerfully. The Corinthians were examples of giving, yet they were not wealthy people. Instead, even out of their poverty, they gave cheerfully (see 2 Cor. 8:1–5; 9:6–8).

We Give Faithfully. Hezekiah urged the people to give and indeed "they faithfully brought in the contributions, tithes and dedicated gifts" (2 Chron. 31:12).

We Give Systematically. Paul urged the Corinthians to bring their offerings "on the first day of every week" (1 Cor. 16:2). If we get paid every two weeks, bring it every two weeks. If we get paid once a month, then use that frequency. A farmer may only receive money once or twice a year. Whatever our circumstances, it is wise to form habits of being consistent and systematic in our giving.

We Give Devotedly. Paul makes a keen insight into the Corinthians' devotion to God when he tells us that "they gave themselves first to the Lord" (2 Cor. 8:5). This is the best motivation for all giving, out of devotion and commitment to the Lord.

Including the 90 Percent

It would be easy to read the previous paragraphs and think that stewardship is only about what we do with the 10 percent or the tithe. Actually, if a person earns $1,000, it isn't just $100 that belongs to God. All of it belongs to Him!

Therefore we must be good stewards of the 90 percent as well. We should manage finances well, saving and investing wisely and shopping for the best buy on a car or a house or the clothes we wear. We should wean ourselves from dependence on credit cards and learn to live within our means so we don't misuse the resources God has entrusted into our hands.

Good financial planners often recommend that we use the following method to allocate our income and expenditures:

1. Give 10 percent to God through the Church.
2. Save 10 percent through savings or investments.
3. Use 80 percent for living expenses.

In these days when credit is easy to get and hard to get rid of, high debt loads often compete with the concept of tithing. Many people are financially strapped due to bad habits relating to their use of money. The idea of paying out 10 percent to the church when they have difficulty paying their bills is not attractive. However, when we realize that God has both commanded and commended tithing, we will want to begin to take steps to bring our lives into obedience to His plan

> God's promises to the person who tithes faithfully are very real.

for our finances. Paying off high interest debt is a good first step. Along with that, we can begin to give as much as possible to God through the Church, making it our goal to tithe. Then stretch beyond the tithe to give special offerings as soon as possible. We will find from our own experiences that God's promises to the person who tithes faithfully are very real.

Do you tithe your income? If not, what steps will you take to develop this practice?

Practical Reasons for Stewardship

There are some very practical reasons for practicing Christian stewardship in both our church and our community.

Kingdom Expansion

Those who object to tithing are faced with the burden of finding a better way to reach people for Christ. Those who object to the use of spiritual gifts are faced with the burden of finding a better way to equip people to serve God so that His kingdom advances. Those who object to investing their time for God and the Church are faced with the burden of finding some better way to tap into the vast human resources that are so valuable for God's kingdom. The local church depends on the faithful investment of time, talent, and treasure on the part of its members.

People Development

God is not just in the business of maintaining the ecclesiastical structure of the Church. He is also in the business of developing us into the people He wants us to be. By the careful use of our time, the cheerful use of our gifts, and the consistent use of our finances, we grow into spiritual maturity as people who are committed to Him.

Community Blessing

As Christians we have a responsibility to make a positive impact on our community. If our gifts would indicate an ability to serve on the city council or a charitable organization in the community, that is a valid way to serve. We may also be involved on school boards, PTAs, and committees of the local school that enable us to have a positive influence on the educational process. Many communities have crisis pregnancy centers, addiction recovery ministries, hospice, and other ministries where we can use our spiritual gifts. A Christian witness, offered lovingly and non-judgmentally, can have a beneficial, even redemptive, impact on one's neighbors and other people in the community.

One caution: we always have to face the issue of balance. How much time do we give to the community without neglecting our family and active participation in our local church? How much money do we invest in charitable causes in the community without depriving our church of the tithe it deserves? How much involvement in church and community is appropriate in the light of our family responsibilities? These are issues that each Christian must sort out in the interest of good stewardship.

How are you currently involved in the life of your local church?
How are you currently involved in your community?

Results of Stewardship

Each Christian must commit to living a life of careful stewardship. We must develop an attitude of obedience to God regarding the use of our time, talent, and treasure. Someone has observed that the last place of resistance to fall is the purse or wallet.

John Wesley knew that giving to the Lord is but transporting our goods to a higher level. He said, "When I have any money, I get rid of it as quickly as possible, lest it find a way into my heart."

Our goal is to become not just givers of money, but giving people. Paul said, "Whoever sows sparingly will also reap sparingly, and whoever sows generously will also reap generously" (2 Cor. 9:6). While he said this in the context of financial giving, it is a great principle for life. By giving generously of our time and talents, as well as our treasures, we will discover it all comes back to us. As Jesus said, "Give, and it will be given to you. A good measure, pressed down, shaken together and running over, will be poured into your lap. For with the measure you use, it will be measured to you" (Luke 6:38).

Someone asked Gen. William Booth, founder of the Salvation Army, what had been the secret of his success. He said, "I will tell you the secret. God has had all there was of me to have. There have been men with greater opportunities; but from the day I got the poor of London on my heart, and a vision of what Jesus Christ could do, I made up my mind that God would have all there was of William Booth. And if there is anything of power in the Salvation Army today, it is because God has had all the adoration of my heart, all the power of my will, and all the influence of my life."

That is stewardship at its finest!

On a scale of 1–10, with 1 meaning no commitment and 10 meaning total commitment, how would you rate yourself in stewardship of time, talent, and treasure?

Time

| 1 | 2 | 3 | 4 | 5 | 6 | 7 | 8 | 9 | 10 |

Talent

| 1 | 2 | 3 | 4 | 5 | 6 | 7 | 8 | 9 | 10 |

Treasure

| 1 | 2 | 3 | 4 | 5 | 6 | 7 | 8 | 9 | 10 |

What are your goals for stewardship of time, talent, and treasure?

To Learn More

The Complete Financial Guide for Young Couples by Larry Burkett

Giving: Unlocking the Heart of Good Stewardship by John Ortberg

Homebuilders Couples: Mastering Money in Your Marriage by Ron Blue

Your Child and Money: A Family Activity Book by Larry Burkett

Master Your Money by Ron Blue

All additional books and resources are available from Wesleyan Publishing House at www.wesleyan.org/wph or by calling 800.4.WESLEY (800.493.7539).

Personal Spiritual Journal

DATE _____

_____

_____

_____

_____

_____

_____

_____

_____

_____

_____

_____

_____

My Prayer Today—

_____

_____

_____

_____

CHAPTER 3

Habits of a Healthy Heart

Spiritual Disciplines

> *And whatever you do, whether in word or deed, do it all in the name of the Lord Jesus, giving thanks to God the Father through him.*
>
> —Colossians 3:17

 **Bible Basics**

Colossians 3:12–17

[12]Therefore as God's chosen people, holy and dearly loved, clothe yourselves with compassion, kindness, humility, gentleness and patience. [13]Bear with each other and forgive whatever grievances you may have against one another. Forgive as the Lord forgave you. [14]And over all these virtues put on love, which binds them all together in perfect unity. [15]Let the peace of Christ rule in your hearts, since as members of one body you were called to peace. And be thankful. [16]Let the word of Christ dwell in you richly as you teach and admonish one another with all wisdom, and as you sing psalms, hymns and spiritual songs with gratitude in your hearts to God. [17]And whatever you do, whether in word or deed, do it all in the name of the Lord Jesus, giving thanks to God the Father through him.

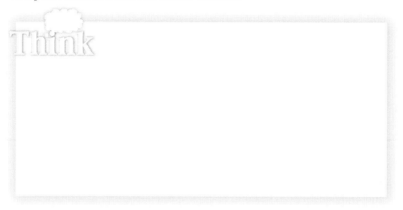 Connecting God's Word to Life

What changes would you need to make in your life to fully obey the instructions in these verses?

Spiritual Disciplines

Living the life that Paul describes in Col. 3:12–17 doesn't happen by accident. It requires a life transformation. Christians must make choices that develop godly character and build spiritual discipline. Marked by self-control—the essence of discipline—we can flourish in a positive, growing relationship with God and with other believers.

Historically, Christians have found certain *spiritual disciplines* (plural) to be essential in cultivating the spiritual life. These disciplines boil down to the choices Christians make to enact behaviors that foster spiritual vitality and holy living.

But spiritual disciplines are not an end in themselves. No spiritual practice possesses magic or inherent merit. The goal of the spiritual disciplines is not to live a regimented life but rather to have a relationship with the Living God through Jesus, His Son. Spiritual disciplines simply provide the framework within which a personal relationship with God flourishes. (Remember Phil. 3:2–11 and Col. 2:6–23.)

Colossians 3:17 illustrates this God focus. We offer literally *all* of our activity to God so that all we do reflects well on the name of Jesus. That is, we choose to live in a manner that is immersed in the spirit of Jesus. Often we must choose to live "in the name of Jesus" against our natural inclination and contrary to cultural pressure. We are enabled to do this by the Holy Spirit, who cultivates the fruit of self-control within us. This isn't something we can do on our own. (Check Col. 1:9–23.) Yet our choices place us into the stream of God's grace, which powerfully carries us along.

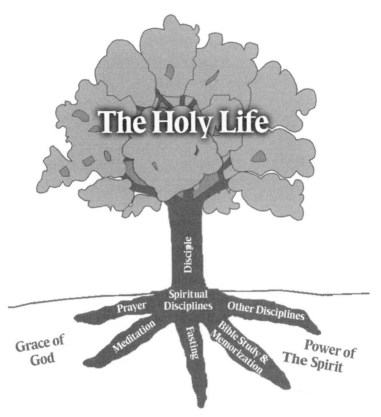

Prayer

Prayer is the spiritual discipline basic to life in Christ, because prayer directly engages us with God. Prayer specifically involves talking *with* God. This entails talking *to* God. It also includes listening as God talks *to us*. Without this communication and communion with God, there is no spiritual life in the first place or development of it on the journey.

Kinds of Prayer

The book of Psalms teaches us just how rich and varied the sorts of conversations we will have with the Lord in prayer can be.

Petitions. For many people "prayer" means asking God for help, and understandably so. Life with God in Christ can begin with asking God to forgive our sin, to have mercy on us, or to rescue us from a pit we have dug. Many psalms record this sort of conversation with God. Psalm 67 is a good example of routine requests and Psalms 3 and 7 illustrate desperate cries for help. The psalmists thought no topic or need was outside of God's range of interest and power. Thus they encourage us to bring all of our needs to God in prayer. But confining prayer to this asking of God to meet our needs severely limits communion with God, in spite of its importance.

Praise. Sometimes the psalmists praised God for His goodness to them. See Psalm 30. Often prayer affirmed renewed or historic trust in God, making claims about their

> We gain clarity or conviction by talking over issues with our Maker and Redeemer.

relationship with God or about what God has done in their lives (as in Psalm 31). At times the psalmists' prayers are primarily praise or thanksgiving and reflection on God's character or the amazing things He has done in history. Think of Psalm 8: "O LORD . . . how majestic is your name in all the earth! . . . When I consider your heavens, the work of your fingers, . . . what is man that you are mindful of him." (Psalms 9 and 90 are similar.)

Reflection. Many prayers in the Psalms mull over a topic in the presence of God. Of course we aren't informing God, but we gain clarity or conviction by talking over issues with our Maker and Redeemer. Psalm 139 is a premier example of this reflective prayer. Here the pondering leads finally to petition.

Questions. A number of powerful prayers in the Psalms ask God questions about topics on which He sometimes seems silent. "Why? How long? When?" These questions usually regard God's response to human need, especially suffering. See how the psalmists pour out their heart to God in Psalms 10, 74, and 89:38–52. People can only venture to have this kind of conversation with a Person big enough and trustworthy enough to "take it."

Confession. Some of the best known Psalms are prayers of confession. The Psalmists bared their souls before God, admitting what they had done and pondering the causes and consequences of their sins. These confessions, like Psalm 51, often cry out, not only for forgiveness, but also for the full range of restoration in the Spirit. It is important to remember that confession of sin is appropriate for all believers.

Mixed Modes. Many prayers in Psalms mix several of these conversational modes together according to the situation at hand. Psalm 71 is an example of these prayers that blend petition, praise, testimony, questions, reflection, and more into a single prayer. These mixed prayers probably reflect most accurately the sort of variegated conversation we will have with God.

The breadth of our prayer interests provides one measure of our spiritual maturity. Research has shown that most people pray, Christian and non-Christian alike. And they pray generally for the same things: help with family, finances, job, protection, and the like. People growing in Christ will learn to branch out beyond this standard *want list*. Our orientation in prayer should shift from our own needs to God's praise, God's kingdom, and the accomplishment of His will on earth.

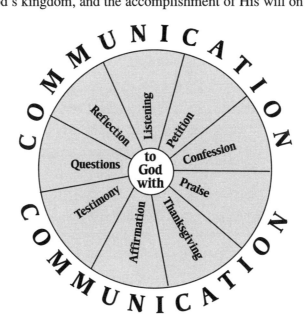

The Goal of Prayer

A personal relationship with God in Christ amounts to knowing God in the person of Jesus Christ. Knowing God is different from knowing *about* God. Knowing God inevitably entails knowing about God. But the reverse is not necessarily the case! Two powerful statements in the New Testament underscore this priority. Jesus Himself said of the Father, "Now this is eternal life: that they may *know you*, the only true God, and Jesus Christ, whom you have sent" (John 17:3). Paul remarked of his own unending spiritual quest, "I want to *know Christ* and the power of His resurrection and the fellowship of sharing in His sufferings, becoming like Him. . ." (Phil. 3:10–11).

In some ways we get to know God in the same way we get to know any other person. It's easy to see that an occasional prayer about the miscellaneous needs of life will not help us much in our quest to know God. Knowing God in Jesus requires ongoing, regular communication, just like knowing another human being requires this. We can learn more about someone by reading about them and asking others about them. That is why, in the process of learning about God, we study Scripture and discuss our spiritual journey with others. But these good activities won't actually translate into knowing God Himself unless we also attend to God in prayer.

Habits of Prayer

Since the only way we can truly know God is by spending consistent time in His presence, the spiritual discipline of prayer helps us to build this habit into our lifestyle. Fruitful habits of prayer have several characteristics.

Long-term. We begin a life long conversation with God, committing to be together from now on, praying daily and throughout every day. This is not just a New Year's resolution or something we try on for size. The format of our discipline of prayer with God may vary with the ebb and flow of life and health, but will be there year after year in some fashion.

Scheduled. We need regularly scheduled times for tending to our spiritual life: time for prayer, meditation, confession, service, study, and other spiritual disciplines. Usually a daily schedule proves to be most practical and life changing. Some people prefer scheduling time every other day because of work or family obligations. Others have more success at protecting one evening or one morning a week for a more extended time of prayer, study, and meditation. It is not for others to dictate this schedule. But if our definition of "regular" turns out to be once a month or once a quarter, it ceases to be much of a discipline.

> Knowing God requires ongoing, regular communication.

Recorded. A spiritual life journal or notebook can help us to keep track of our prayer life: requests, answers, topics of concern, things learned. We refer to this practice as journal writing.

Earlier we raised the notion that prayer and knowing God are not just talking to God. Communication with God involves having God speak to us and cultivating the habit of listening to God. This journal becomes our record of our ongoing conversation with God.

Confirmed. God speaks most clearly to us in Scripture, as we read over the shoulder of people to whom God spoke long ago. God also speaks to us through Christian counsel, that is, through consultation and conversation with other disciples of Jesus (and sometimes nonbelievers). God also speaks through music and art and creation.

Which type of prayer have you used the most? Why?

Meditation

Prayer leads us into a second spiritual discipline called *meditation*. Meditation is the spiritual discipline of thinking about a given matter carefully, reflectively, and pondering or musing over the item at some length. Meditation is not daydreaming or simple stream of consciousness. Like the other disciplines this one rings better as a verb, *to meditate*, because it involves the choice to do something—to think, to "love the Lord with all your *mind*" (Mark 12:28–31, emphasis added).

Meditating is the mechanism by which important matters get processed and brought meaningfully into our lives. People with no time for careful thought are seldom able to integrate into their lives what they have heard preached or taught in church, or what they have read in the Bible. They may have lots of information, but are less likely to know what that information actually means or implies.

The discussion of when to meditate parallels options of when to pray. One can meditate while doing some other tasks—washing dishes, driving a car, jogging, weeding the garden, and other tasks where one's mind can be free to work on other questions. But meditation should be one of those behaviors included in the scheduled time we make for communion with God. Thinking substantially about a matter will generally require some privacy, relative quiet, and freedom from major distractions. (Clearly by these guides and for safety reasons, heavy traffic and crooked roads would not be places to meditate while driving!)

> Meditation involves both asking questions and listening for God's response.

Our meditation will emerge from and feed into other spiritual disciplines and our life in general. Meditating assumes that there is a topic for reflection—some issue, question, subject, mystery, truth, problem, or the like. These topics may come from the news, from our general or academic reading, sacred and secular, from discussions or conversations we enter, from experiences we have, and much more.

Most productive meditation includes two elements: asking thought-provoking questions and listening receptively for God's response.

Topics for Meditation

Simple questions are our best tools in clear thinking as well as in study. What does this word or expression mean—as a dictionary definition and in a fuller sense? What is involved in this? What are its main parts? Why is this as it is? How does this work? If this is true, what must also be true, if we think consistently? What does this already assume? What follows from this? What does this imply? We don't need to be afraid of any question that helps us to understand our faith better or live more obedient lives. God has heard them all by this time. And don't make the mistake of thinking meditation is somehow only for brainy ones in the church or for naturally quiet and contemplative people. These questions can be used by all of us to focus our thinking.

Here are some examples of themes for meditation.

- How can I best demonstrate my loyalty to Christ in my relationship with _____ to whom I seem increasingly committed?

- God, what do You want to teach me through the little one that is growing inside me and will soon be born?

- The pastor said holiness means "belonging completely to Jesus." How would that ripple through my life?

We can ponder teachings also, like those Paul gave to the Colossian church.

- What is the peace of Christ?

- If the peace of Christ ruled in our fellowship, what would be the clues that it was so?

- What does the fact that these people are all members of one body have to do with this ruling of the peace of Christ?

- Why does Paul refer to these people as "holy, chosen and dearly beloved" when they obviously have spiritual ground to take?

- What would increased "compassion, kindness, humility, gentleness and patience" look like in my life?

- If I forgive _____, what changes would that bring to our neighborhood?

- Why does Paul claim that love binds all other virtues together?

- Paul says "whatever you do . . . in word or in deed, do it all in the name of the Lord Jesus." What do I tend to say or do that doesn't reflect well on the name of Jesus?

The Response to Meditation

Meditating is not only about answering questions or solving problems. Obviously answers do come, and problems do get solved. But meditation is more about considering and pondering these items in the presence of God and letting solutions emerge, or suggestions arise, or possibilities percolate. Meditation sends us to other resources for study, to other people for consultation, and to our knees for surrender and commitment.

Meditation is not primarily about listening to God, as we have already seen. Indeed it is broader than that. But prayer and meditation surely are two places for listening to God.

> In prayer and meditation we listen to God *implicitly*.

In prayer and meditation we listen to God *implicitly*. That is, while we are actually about the business of praying for various matters and meditating on questions, we may discover God speaking to us. His voice is heard implicitly in the very process of prayer and meditation. At other times we will listen to God *intentionally*. We have prayed; we have meditated. Now we sit silently, open to the voice of God. We are not hurried. We have no particular expectations. We wait for the voice of God in our heart. This overlaps into the separate spiritual discipline of silence, but I think we are not far afield here to link it directly to prayer and now to meditation.

We should not claim that what God has said to us He necessarily applies to everyone. And we should not rush to the conclusion that God has spoken a given word to us. The church can help us to evaluate what we think we have heard using Scripture, reason, experience, and tradition (i.e., the collected wisdom of the historic and contemporary church). Nevertheless, having said all of this, the people of God have discovered that as they listen for the voice of God He will speak to them over time. Meditation can provide a fertile place for this listening to God.

Think of a Bible verse that has puzzled or troubled you. What are your questions about that Scripture? Find a time to sit quietly and meditate about the implications of that verse for your situation.

Fasting

Considering the alarming rate of obesity in the North American church we might think fasting should be a mandatory spiritual discipline, beginning in the toddlers' class. But fasting as a spiritual discipline is not primarily about controlling our weight or maintaining physical health. A spiritual commitment to be a good steward of the body God has given us could lead to fasting, but fasting is more than just going on a diet.

Fasting is the voluntary choice to abstain from eating all or certain foods for a set period of time. Other kinds of fasts include abstaining from sexual relationships, from favorite activities, hobbies, entertainments, or other items for the sake of focusing our full attention on Christ. We will discuss abstaining from solid foods.

Fasting from food generally does not exclude the intake of fluids and should not include omitting prescribed medicines or the food necessary to take them! People should never "fast" from prescribed medicines. Those on prescribed diets or continuing medications that essentially control symptoms and make healthy life possible (people with diabetes, high blood pressure, seizures, and the like) should consult their physician before fasting.

> Spiritual disciplines have value only in the context of a relationship with God.

The tradition of fasting began centuries before the birth of Christ. People have used fasting as a way of expressing deeply felt emotions over spiritual transactions, often sorrow or regret (Joel 2:12–14), or of marking particularly memorable and often difficult events (Zech. 7:2–5; 8:18–19). Over time people began to think of fasting as a way of gaining recognition from God and fellow believers. Jesus soundly rejected the notion that fasting itself had any particular merit (Luke 18:9–14). He insisted that fasting and other acts of spiritual discipline were transactions between people and God, of value only for the sake of and in the course of an authentic relationship with God. They were not meant to impress God or others (Matt. 6:1–18, especially vv. 16–18).

But Jesus clearly did assume His followers would fast. In Matt. 6:16 He said, "When you fast. . . ." not "If you fast. . . ." There are many reasons Christians choose to fast. It is a way to elevate spiritual nourishment above matters of physical sustenance. It helps us to give marked attention to the life, death, and resurrection of Jesus—especially at times of the year such as Lent. It is a means of focusing on our life with God in Christ over all other matters. It makes time available to practice the other spiritual disciplines. Fasting can also be a way of expressing solidarity with believers around the world who lack sufficient food or who are undergoing suffering.

Though fasting is not primarily about "pummeling our bodies into submission" (1 Cor. 9:27), it is part of learning self-control, the essence of spiritual discipline. So if our first reaction to the thought of fasting is that we could not possibly give up lunch or dinner, that alone might indicate that we could benefit from this discipline. We could fast as an expression of our desire to "seek first the Kingdom" if for no other reason (Matt. 6:33).

Fasting involves more than simply refraining from eating. Eating occupies much of our time. The time that we free up by fasting should be spent in prayer, meditation, study, or service in keeping with the goal of our fast. One might think that going without food would prove anything but helpful in focusing our attention beyond food. Surprisingly, this is usually not the case, especially when we become more experienced. Some people fast occasionally, others by the church calendar (Lent), and others on a regular basis (one meal or one day or more a week).

Have you ever fasted as a spiritual discipline? What was the goal of your fast?

Bible Study and Memorization

Perhaps the most important reason spiritual discipline always includes Scripture study and memorization is this: The Holy Spirit uses our study of the Word of God not only to inform us, but also to transform us into the image of Christ. Scripture gives us the surest account of the will of God, the clearest picture of the person of Jesus, and the most secure expectations for life in the Spirit.

By *study* we mean to include a variety of intentional readings of Scripture. Like the other disciplines, Bible study changes with the ebb and flow of life and with our growth in the faith. There are times when we need to read rapidly and generally to get the big picture, covering book after book of the Bible in a survey sort of reading. This survey gives us an indispensable grasp of the whole story and helps us to situate ourselves within that story. At other times we should pay extended attention to a single book such as Genesis, Matthew, or Romans, or a group of books, like the Pentateuch, the Gospels, or the Epistles. Within these books we can pause to dig deeply into specific, key passages. As with other aspects of spiritual discipline, we are aiming here for the long haul in Bible study. Remember Ps. 1; 119:10; and 2 Tim. 3:14–16.

Orientation for Bible Study

Study the Bible in units. Aim not just to know verses but to become familiar with the basic content and flow of books as whole. For instance, even though John 3:16 is a blessed promise, it is even more wonderful when understood within the context of the rest of the gospel of John. Beginners would do well to start with Luke, Acts, Ephesians, and Genesis. This plan covers the life of Jesus, the history and teachings of the early Church, and the Creator-Redeemer.

Basic equipment for Bible study includes keeping a notebook to record our insights (you may choose to use part of your journal for notes). This signals seriousness about our work. Scripture will be more understandable if we refer to several versions of the Bible including some reputable, contemporary paraphrases. A good concordance and Bible dictionary will also come in handy.

It is helpful to adopt a mind-set of first putting ourselves in the world of the ancient readers—a world without electricity, without automobiles, computers, plastics, hypodermics, germs, viruses, or democracies as we know them. Then ponder how the Word given to them applies to our modern situation.

Directions for Bible Study

Entering Scripture study as a spiritual discipline is like getting on a metro subway loop. We can enter at any one of a number of points. But if we stay on the train, we will eventually stop at all the stations. The "stations" on the Scripture study loop are consecration, content, concept, canon, and connection.

Bible Study Loop

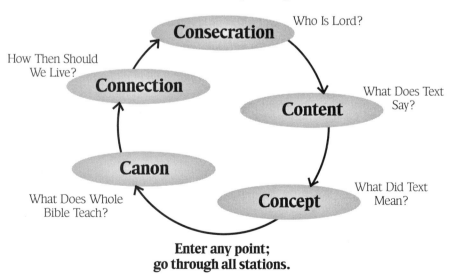

Enter any point;
go through all stations.

Life positions us to enter at different stations on the Scripture study loop. No matter where we enter, life long Scripture study should pass through all the stops on the loop with all of Scripture.

Consecration. Who is Lord in my life as I study? The best way to begin and end our time in Scripture is by surrendering ourselves to Christ, the Living Word, asking for a teachable heart, and committing ourselves to apply what we learn.

> The best way to begin reading Scripture is to surrender ourselves to Christ.

Content. What exactly does the text say and how does it fit together? This is the stage for observation. Start by seeing the overview of the book or chapter. Then move to the parts. In short books give brief titles to the paragraphs; gather two to five paragraphs into segments and title these segments, and then give a title to the book as a whole. For longer books, move directly to titling chapters. Then gather chapters into divisions and finally title the book.

Observe the flow of thought in the book, passage, or paragraph. Does the unit have an introduction? What topics are introduced? Is there a turning point or a set of contrasting ideas? What questions are posed? How are themes developed to a climax? Spotting these elements will strengthen our grasp of the Word.

Concept. What does the text mean? Ask what the material meant to its early readers. At this stage we begin to draw conclusions to interpret the text. For example, what did Paul mean by "the gospel of Christ" in Rom. 1:16? How is it the "power of God to salvation?" And how would Paul have defined the word *salvation*? Then look for answers to these questions by studying the book of Romans itself further and by consulting trusted resources.

Canon. What does the Bible as a whole teach on this issue? We can use a concordance, a topical Bible, or the cross-reference section of our Bible to locate other Bible passages that address the same issues as the passage we are studying. Listen to the conversation God has inspired on given topics in the Bible as a whole. The Spirit will enable us to discern *how* our passage fits into that conversation and how it speaks cross-culturally to us today. If our conclusions are correct, they will be reinforced throughout the rest of Scripture.

Connection. How should I apply this text to my life? Now that we have discovered what the Bible says and what it means, it is time to apply it to our situation. Questions can help here too. How does this teaching affirm, correct, and inform us? What sins should we confess? What specific choices should be made regarding our resources—property, time, money, reputation, health, influence, and more? What affirmation or revision of faith or values should we make? We should think of applications both individually and corporately. In this life long process the Word will shape us.

Memorization of Scripture

When we find a text that speaks powerfully to us, we should memorize it. This could be the key verse of a section or a passage that speaks pointedly to our situation. Writing the text over several times, speaking it as we write it, will help us in the memory process. Many people find it helpful to post passages in prominent places such as on steering wheels, mirrors, exercise machines, workbenches—any place conducive to review of the passage. Once we get comfortable memorizing short passages, we will be greatly blessed if we branch out to memorize short books such as Colossians or Philippians or famous passages like the Sermon on the Mount. If we set a pace such as a verse or paragraph a week, it is an easily achievable goal. The key verse of each chapter in this book may help you begin memorizing. The verses are printed on perforated cards at the back of the book.

What could you do to become more systematic in your study of the Word?

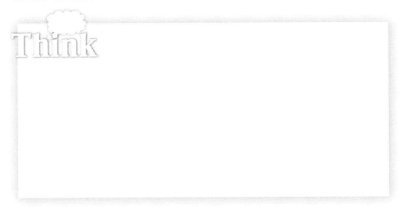

Your Spiritual Ammunition

The spiritual disciplines of vital prayer, meditation, fasting, Bible study, and Scripture memorization provide our best ammunition against the Enemy. Recall that the only offensive weapon in Paul's description of the armor of God is the Word of God (Eph 6:17). The effectiveness of the disciplines lies in the fact that they cultivate our relationship with the living Christ Himself, just as the best defense against marital unfaithfulness is a satisfying relationship with our spouse. Our relationship with Christ actually constitutes the mainframe for the whole "weapons system" of the believer, without which "ammunition" proves useless or ineffective.

The disciplines are best practiced within a healthy Christian community. Our meaningful participation in a local church, regular study of His Word in a Sunday School class or small group, plus fellowship with a group of friends who will hold us accountable is essential. This is our best ammunition against excess or error. The choices Paul encourages as life habits of godliness in Col. 3:15–17 are choices to be made *by* a group and *in* a group. It is wise to cultivate relationships with people who will support our life of prayer, Scripture study, memorization, meditation, fasting, and other Christian disciplines. These fellow believers can pray for and with us and ask us the hard questions that will keep us honest and growing in the Lord.

Who do you know who regularly practices these disciplines? What could you do to cultivate a supportive relationship with them?

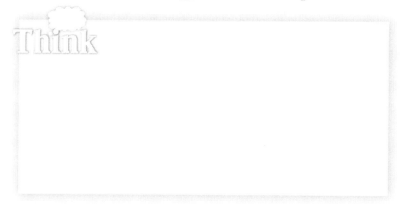

To Learn More

Bible Study That Works by David L. Thompson

The Book of Common Prayer

Celebration of Discipline by Richard J. Foster

Discover the Word edited by Everett Leadingham

Shaped by the Word by Robert Mulholland

All additional books and resources are available from Wesleyan Publishing House at www.wesleyan.org/wph or by calling 800.4.WESLEY (800.493.7539).

Personal Spiritual Journal

DATE _____

_____

_____

_____

_____

_____

_____

_____

_____

_____

_____

_____

_____

_____

My Prayer Today—

_____

_____

_____

_____

CHAPTER 4

The Mystery of God

The Trinity

*Therefore go and make disciples of all nations, baptizing
them in the name of the Father and of the Son and of the
Holy Spirit. . . .*

—Matthew 28:19

 **Bible Basics**

Matthew 3:13–17

[13]Then Jesus came from Galilee to the Jordan to be baptized by John. [14]But John
tried to deter him, saying, "I need to be baptized by you, and do you come to
me?" [15]Jesus replied, "Let it be so now; it is proper for us to do this to fulfill all
righteousness." Then John consented. [16]As soon as Jesus was baptized, He went
up out of the water. At that moment heaven was opened, and He saw the Spirit
of God descending like a dove and lighting on him. [17]And a voice from heaven
said, "This is my Son, whom I love; with him I am well pleased."

Matthew 28:18–20

[18]Then Jesus came to them and said, "All authority in heaven and on earth has
been given to me. [19]Therefore go and make disciples of all nations, baptizing
them in the name of the Father and of the Son and of the Holy Spirit, [20]and
teaching them to obey everything I have commanded you. And surely I am
with you always, to the very end of the age."

2 Corinthians 13:14

> May the grace of the Lord Jesus Christ, and the love of God, and the fellowship of the Holy Spirit be with you all.

 **Connecting God's Word to Life**

Circle the references to the Father, Son, and Holy Spirit in each of the three passages. What do these references tell you about what God is like?

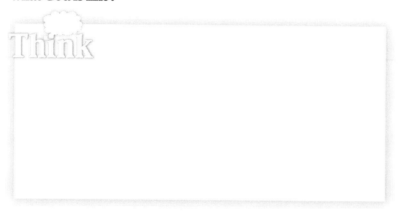

The Mystery of the Trinity

The Bible says that God is one—and yet three! This notion is called the doctrine of the Trinity. Simply, it means that God is three persons yet is one. Reginald Heber has expressed this truth eloquently in one of the great hymns of the faith.

> Holy, holy, holy! Lord God almighty!
> All Thy works shall praise Thy name in earth and sky and sea.
> Holy, holy, holy! Merciful and mighty!
> God in three persons, blessed Trinity! Amen.

How did Christians arrive at this unique concept of God? How did this doctrine develop in the early church? Why is it stated in the way that it is? This belief is clearly founded in the both the New Testament and the Old Testament and was the firmly held belief of the earliest Christians.

The Witness of the New Testament

First, let's take a look at what the Christian Scripture, the New Testament of the Bible, has to say about the Trinity.

Evidence for the Oneness of God

The oneness of God is stated very clearly in the New Testament. In Jesus' high priestly prayer for His disciples the night before the crucifixion, He said to the Father, "Now this is eternal life: that they may know You, the only true God, and Jesus Christ, whom You have sent" (John 17:3). Paul also repeatedly emphasized the oneness: "Yet for us there is but one God, the Father, from whom all things came and for whom we live; and there is but one Lord, Jesus Christ, through whom all things came and through whom we live" (1 Cor. 8:6). "There is one body and one Spirit—just as you were called to one hope when you were called—one Lord, one faith, one baptism; one God and Father of all, who is over all and through all and in all" (Eph. 4:4–6).

Evidence for the Threeness of God

The threeness of God is also revealed in the New Testament. The first of our key passages, Matt. 3:13–17, tells the story of Jesus' baptism, the public act which marked the beginning of His public ministry. As Jesus came up out of the water, heaven was opened and the Spirit of God descended like a dove and settled on Him. Also the Father spoke from heaven saying, "This is my Son, whom I love; with him I am well pleased." All three Persons were present in one scene.

The second key passage, Matt. 28:18–20, contains the story of one of Jesus' appearances to His followers after His resurrection shortly before He ascended into heaven. He gave them the Great Commission, commanding them to "go and make disciples of all nations, baptizing them in the name of the Father and of the Son and of the Holy Spirit."

The third key passage, 2 Cor. 13:14, is the benediction with which Paul closed his second letter to the Corinthians. The

> "May the grace of the Lord Jesus Christ, and the love of God, and the fellowship of the Holy Spirit be with you all" (2 Cor. 13:14).

church has used this great benediction ever since Paul's day. "May the grace of the Lord Jesus Christ, and the love of God, and the fellowship of the Holy Spirit be with you all."

Many other New Testament passages could be cited. One is Peter's greeting to the people to whom he wrote his first epistle. It is addressed to those "who have been chosen according to the foreknowledge of God the Father, through the sanctifying work of the Spirit, for obedience to Jesus Christ and sprinkling by his blood" (1 Pet. 1:2).

Evidence That Jesus Is God

The threeness is further emphasized in the New Testament by the fact that both the Father and Jesus are called God. In Matt. 1:23, the angel tells Joseph that the child to be born will be called "'Immanuel'—which means, 'God with us.'" In John 1:1–3, we read, "In the beginning was the Word, and the Word was with God, and the Word was God. He was with God in the beginning. Through Him all things were made; without Him nothing was made that has been made." John makes it clear in the following verses that he is speaking of Jesus, climaxing it in John 1:18, "No one has ever seen God, but God the One and Only, who is at the Father's side, has made Him known." In Rom. 9:5, Paul speaks of "Christ, who is God over all." In Titus 2:13, Paul said that we are awaiting "the glorious appearing of our great God and Savior, Jesus Christ." And in Peter's introduction to his second epistle he addressed "those who through the righteousness of our God and Savior Jesus Christ have received a faith as precious as ours" (2 Pet. 1:1).

Evidence That the Holy Spirit Is God

Once the Scriptures have made clear that the Father is God and that Jesus Christ is God, it becomes obvious from our key passages that the Holy Spirit is also God. He is given equal prominence as the other two at Jesus' baptism, in the baptismal formula, and in Paul's benediction. Even more significantly, three times in the New Testament a reference is made to the Holy Spirit, citing an Old Testament passage that refers to the one God Yahweh or Jehovah (LORD).

Compare These Old Testament and New Testament Passages.		
Old Testament	New Testament	Comparison
Isa. 6:5–10	Acts 28:25–27	
Exod. 17:7	Heb. 3:7–9	
Jer. 31:31–34	Heb. 10:15–17	

How do the Scriptures cited help you to understand the idea of God as Three-in-One?

The Witness of the Old Testament

We looked at the New Testament first because its testimony to God's threeness in God's oneness is quite clear and explicit. From that perspective we now look at the Old Testament. While the Old Testament does not make such open and explicit references to the Trinity, there are many passages that imply a plurality within God's singleness.

Evidence for the Oneness of God

The great passage on God's oneness is Deuteronomy 6:4, "Hear, O Israel: The LORD our God, the LORD is one." This verse is part of Israel's *Shema*, the confession of faith recited by devout Jews each morning and each evening.

Evidence for the Threeness of God

Possible references to the threeness of God occur as early as Gen. 1. Genesis 1:1 uses the Hebrew name *Elohim* to identify the God who created. This word is a plural form and could be translated "gods." It was used in its plural form to refer to the Hebrew's God, also known by the Hebrew *Yahweh* or *Jehovah*. Hebrew grammarians explained that the word *Elohim* was a "plural of majesty, a plural of powers, or an intensive plural." But the possibility that the plural form implies more is heightened by other considerations in Gen. 1. "God" is often used in the New Testament to refer specifically to the Father. And if we think of the Father as the Creator in Gen. 1:1, we find also that "the Spirit of God was hovering over the waters" (1:2), and that it was the spoken Word that brought light (and every other thing) into existence (1:3). John identifies Jesus as the Word in the opening verses of his gospel. We find another hint of God's threeness in Gen. 1:26 when Elohim (God in plural form) says, "Let *us* make man in *our* image, in *our* likeness." After Adam's fall in Eden, "the LORD God said, 'The man has now become like one of *us*, knowing good and evil'" (Gen. 3:22). And when Noah's descendants were building the tower of Babel, the Lord said, "Come, let *us* go down and confuse their language" (Gen. 11:7—italics added in all three quotations).

Isaiah contains strong implications of God's threeness. During his transforming vision in the Temple in Isa. 6, he quotes the Lord as saying, "Whom shall *I* send? And who will go for *us*?" (6:8; the italics call attention to both the singular "I" and the plural "us"—threeness in oneness). In this context, the threefold cry of the seraphs may well be a hint of praise to the three persons of the Trinity, "Holy, holy, holy is the LORD Almighty" (6:3). In Isa. 61:1, the coming Messiah declares, "The Spirit of the Sovereign LORD is on me, because the LORD has anointed me." Here we may have the Father as the Sovereign Lord, and the Holy Spirit as the Spirit of the Sovereign Lord. The "me" in this prophecy is the Son. Jesus made that clear when He read this passage in the synagogue at Nazareth and claimed to be its fulfillment (Luke 4:16–21).

> The cry of the seraphs is a clue to the Trinity, "Holy, holy, holy . . ." (Isa. 6:3).

References to Christ

In addition to all of these, there are also several probable references to Christ in the Old Testament, particularly those to the "angel of the LORD," the "angel of God," and the "messenger of the covenant." The "angel of the LORD" appeared to Moses in the burning bush (Exod. 3:2), yet the one speaking to Moses is sometimes also called "LORD" and "God." It is clear in Mal. 3:1 that the "messenger [same Hebrew word as *angel*] of the covenant" and the "Lord" are one and the same and that both refer to Christ.

References to the Holy Spirit

The Spirit is mentioned many times in the Old Testament as the "Spirit of the LORD," the "Spirit of God" and even as the "Holy Spirit" (compare Judg. 14:6, 19; 15:14; 1 Sam. 11:6; Isa. 63:10, 11).

How do these Scriptures from the Old Testament strengthen for you the evidence for God as Three-in-One?

The Witness of the Early Church

What we have observed so far is very interesting. The Scriptures declare that God is one, yet they allude to His threeness, implicitly in the Old Testament and explicitly in the New Testament. But there is no systematic attempt to explain how God can be one and three at the same time.

You may have noticed that in our study of the Scriptures, we have not found any references to Trinity or to persons. Yet we use these terms. How did the early church move from the biblical statements to more formal doctrinal statements?

Development of Doctrines

The creeds and other doctrinal statements were not imposed on the church out of the blue by abstract theologians. Virtually every doctrine that was eventually accepted as orthodox (correct doctrine as recognized by the church) developed because some thinker proposed an interpretation of Scripture that the majority did not believe to be correct. In other words, the teaching of heresy (doctrine differing from that generally accepted by the church) unwittingly benefited the church by clarifying the search for the truth.

Early Creeds and Doctrinal Statements

Even during the first century, while the New Testament was being written, the church was developing short, simple doctrinal statements, most of them dealing with who Jesus was. (Possible examples are 1 Cor. 15:3–4; Eph. 4:4–6; Phil. 2:5–11; Col. 1:13–20; 1 Tim. 3:16—this last one is thought by some Bible scholars to be a hymn.) It is obvious that even then there were false teachers. Both Paul and John attempted to answer those who taught errors about Jesus. Some said He was not God and others that He was not man, only a spirit who *appeared* to be a man.

> I believe in God the Father Almighty . . . and in Jesus Christ His only Son our Lord. . . . I believe in the Holy Spirit.

One of the earliest Christian statements of belief appeared in Rome in the second century. It is referred to as the Old Roman Creed. In a somewhat later form, we know and repeat it as the *Apostles' Creed*—although the apostles did not write it.

I believe in God the Father Almighty, Maker of heaven and earth;

And in Jesus Christ His only Son our Lord; who was conceived by the Holy Spirit, born of the Virgin Mary, suffered under Pontius Pilate, was crucified, dead, and buried; He descended into hades; the third day He rose again from the dead; He ascended into heaven, and sitteth at the right hand of God the Father Almighty; from thence He shall come to judge the quick and the dead.

I believe in the Holy Spirit, the holy catholic church, the communion of saints, the forgiveness of sins, the resurrection of the body, and the life everlasting. Amen.

The Creed is essentially an elaboration of the baptismal formula in Matt. 28:19, structured around the three persons of the Trinity, with most of its contents focusing on Jesus Christ, and with a few other matters touched on after reference to the Holy Spirit.

Three Basic Errors

While the New Testament did not explain how God was one and three simultaneously, the attempts of human teachers to reconcile this evidence forced the church to decide what was in harmony with the Scriptures and what was not. There were three basic errors that were expressed in those theories that were eventually condemned as heresies. The first error taught that there was only one indivisible God who showed Himself at different times in three different ways—as the Father (the God of the Old Testament), the Son (Jesus in the New Testament), and the Holy Spirit (who indwelt the church and individual believers). The second error was the subordinating of the Son and the Spirit to the Father in such a way that only the

Father was truly God. And the third error was one that so emphasized the threeness of God that it seemed to say there was not one God but three.

Formulation of the Nicene Creed

The church handled these challenges largely through councils of church leaders called bishops. One met at Nicea in A.D. 325. It expanded the Apostles' Creed into a Nicene Creed. It tackled the issue of the full deity of the Son and concluded by adding more explanation to the statement about Jesus Christ. He was "the only-begotten of His Father before all worlds; God of God, Light of Light, very God of very God; begotten, not made, being of one substance with the Father; by whom all things were made. . . ." The church affirmed that anything less fell short of what the Bible revealed about Jesus.

Following this council, some teachers began to say that there was a "twoness" about God. The Father and the Son were both divine, but the Holy Spirit was not. Another council met at Constantinople in 381 to deal with this faulty doctrine. It expanded the creed a bit more by saying that the Holy Spirit is "the Lord and Giver of Life; who proceeds from the Father and the Son, who with the Father and Son together is worshiped and glorified; who spoke by the prophets." Again the church was convinced that anything less fell short of what the Bible revealed about the Holy Spirit.

If you had been present at the church councils, would you have agreed with the decisions that were made? Why or why not?

The Mystery of the Trinity

It is obvious that the Scriptures made statements that forced the early church to deal theologically with the nature of God as both One and Three. But our minds still struggle with what seem to be mutually exclusive concepts. Why is it so hard for us to understand the Trinity?

Limitations of the Human Mind

The problem is that the human mind cannot possibly comprehend God. We can recognize His existence, see His handiwork, sense His presence, and experience His mercy and grace. But we cannot fully understand Him. We would have to be equal to Him to understand Him. And we are far from being equal to Him. We are His creatures, made in His image, but we are very limited in knowledge, in power, in our orientation to time and space. As Isaiah records, "'For my thoughts are not your thoughts, neither are your ways my ways,' declares the LORD. 'As the heavens are higher than the earth, so are my ways higher than your ways and my thoughts than your thoughts'" (Isa. 55:8–9).

How well do we even understand one another or ourselves? How well do the best scientists understand our universe, our own planet, or even the human mind and body? There are many things which impact our lives physically and emotionally that we only dimly understand. We should not be surprised that there are aspects of God's nature that we cannot get clearly in focus. We see that the Scriptures simultaneously affirm both the oneness and threeness of God. And we can understand something of what drove the early church to seek to define the Trinity sufficiently to avoid errors in understanding. But we still find ourselves between understanding and infinite mystery.

> We should not be surprised that there are aspects of God's nature that we cannot get clearly in focus.

Limited Help from Symbols, Patterns, and Analogies

The church has found some things that help a bit with the mystery. Symbols of the Trinity include the triangle and three interwoven rings. These have been used in religious art, including stained glass windows in churches and cathedrals.

We can find some patterns of three-in-oneness if we look around. The egg is made up of three parts: yolk, white, and shell. A tree has root, trunk, and branches.

Water can be found as liquid, ice, and steam. The sun in our sky is inseparable from the light, which it emits, and the warmth evident wherever its light reaches.

Theologians have used various analogies to ease our intellectual struggle. One is the social analogy. Three human beings can share a common life so closely that they can only be considered as a unity. This is especially evident in a family consisting of a father, a mother, and a child.

> The Father, Son, and Holy Spirit each have a role in our salvation.

Another is the psychological analogy, which attempts to find a faint reflection of three-in-oneness in a human being. One suggestion has been the interaction of mind, emotions, and the will. Somewhat parallel is the suggestion of memory, intelligence, and the will. Paul refers to the "whole spirit, soul and body" (1 Thes. 5:23).

Of course, none of these really unlocks the mystery of God. They can only be suggestive of how three-in-oneness is a viable state of being. They do not explain how God's three-in-oneness operates. As some have put it, it is not that what the Scriptures reveal about God is contrary to reason, but it is above reason—beyond the reach of necessarily limited human reason.

Meaning of Person

One term, which is in the creeds, but not in the Scriptures is *three persons*. It is used for what Kenneth Grider has called "three eternal distinctions in the divine essence."

The word *persons* can be both help and hinder understanding in our present day. The word *person* is from the Latin *persona*. It meant a "mask (especially one worn by an actor), an actor, a role, a character, a person." In our day a person is a totally distinct individual, a personality. If we think of three personalities in the Trinity, we lose the oneness and end up with three gods, which is contrary to Scripture. If we take the mask aspect too far, we think of one God wearing a different mask at different times and we lose the distinctiveness of the three that the Scriptures set forth. It is true that the Father, Son, and Holy Spirit each had a *role* in creation, and each has a *role* in our redemption and in our sanctification. The term *person* is still the best that has been found. The church has hallowed its use through the centuries to distinguish Father, Son, and Holy Spirit within the oneness of God. But we must use it carefully.

Relationships within the Trinity

As we have seen, the Scriptures clearly state that the Father is God, the Son is God, and the Holy Spirit is God. The Scriptures assign the same divine attributes, such as eternity, to each (cf. Deut. 33:27; Heb. 1: 8; 9:14). Yet the Scriptures seem to differentiate between them in their relationship with each other. The Father has a priority within the Trinity, not a priority of time nor a priority of status or ability, but a priority of relationship.

> Father, Son and Spirit are God, yet Scripture differentiates their relationships to each other.

The Father is "the Source of all that exists, whether of matter or spirit." Some Scriptures seem to make the Father the Source of the Son and the Holy Spirit, although *source* in this context cannot mean that there was a time when the Son and the Holy Spirit were not. The Father bears that name in part because of His eternal relation to Christ as the "only begotten Son" (compare the King James Version and the New American Standard Bible translations of John 1:14; 3:16; and Heb. 1:5). This does not mean that the Father is more God than the Son, but somehow the image of a father as the source of a son is like God the Father as the source of God the Son, without there being a beginning point to that relationship. And John 15:26 tells us that the Holy Spirit "goes out" (New International Version) or "proceeds" (King James Version and New American Standard Bible) from the Father. Somehow the image of one in authority sending a representative on a mission is like God the Father eternally being the Source of the Spirit, again without a beginning point in that relationship.

It is implied that the Father sent the Son on His mission to be "God with us" and "God in the flesh." His purpose was to reconcile us to the Father. His present position is "at the Father's right hand," which is a place of honor but not the primary seat on the throne. And it is at God's right hand that He is interceding for us before the Father. Again the picture is of a priority of the Father in relation to the Son.

The Bible sets forth very clearly the full and equal deity of the Holy Spirit. And yet it picks up from John 15:26 that the Spirit "proceeds" from the Father, and it adds "from . . . the Son." Jesus substantiates this, saying that the Father and Son are both involved in sending the Spirit (cf. John 14:16,26; 15:26; 16:7). Jesus said that the Spirit would take what belonged to Jesus and make it known to the disciples (16:13–15). In Rom. 8:9–10, Paul also referred to the Spirit as both the "Spirit of God" and the "Spirit of Christ."

80

In formulating the creeds, the councils always maintained the same order when referring to the Trinity: Father, Son, and Holy Spirit. It appears clear from the Scriptures that these are the first, second, and third members of the Trinity, in order, as a result of the Father's relation to the Son, and the relation of the Father and the Son to the Spirit.

Involvement of the Trinity in Human Need

One truth comes through again and again. No single member of the Trinity, in isolation from the others, ever does any of the great works on behalf of human beings. We already noted that all three were involved in the creation of humans. As to our redemption, the Father expresses His goodwill toward us by seeking and receiving penitent sinners. Jesus stooped to become a man, to die, to rise again, to reconcile us to God, to intercede for us with the Father. And the Spirit is the one who administers grace, effects our conviction, regeneration, sanctification, and glorification—all the results of the Father's loving outreach and Jesus' sacrifice. The Scriptures specify the truth that sanctification is the work of all three (cf. 2 Thes. 2:13; 1 Pet. 1:1–2).

The great benefit of the creeds is that they establish the boundaries. They erect a fence and say, "Within this lies the mystery of the Trinity."[1] This excludes errors. We cannot say less than the Scriptures say, nor less than what the church has arrived at in the creeds. To say more is to venture into risky speculation.

Which of the analogies of the Trinity is most helpful for you? Why?

Worship of the Trinity

A proper understanding of the Trinity will help us in our worship. While prayer to the Son or the Holy Spirit is not wrong, there is only one prayer to the Son in the

New Testament (Acts 7:59) and not one to the Holy Spirit. Jesus taught us that when we pray, we are normally to address "Our Father" (cf. Matt. 6:9; Luke 11:2), and He repeatedly set the example for us. We are to heighten the effectiveness of our prayers by reminding the Father that it is in the Son's name that we pray (John 15:16; 16:23). Jesus intercedes for us and the Holy Spirit helps us pray and also intercedes for us (Rom. 8:26–27, 34).

When we thank and praise and honor the Triune God, it is proper to address the Father and to cite what He and the Son and the Holy Spirit have done and are doing.[2]

The *Gloria Patri* is one of the great aids to worship and sums it all up eloquently.

> Glory be to the Father, and to the Son, and to the Holy Ghost; As it was in the beginning, is now, and ever shall be, world without end. Amen.

We began this lesson circling references in the key passages to the Father, Son, and Holy Spirit and asked what God is like. Now we ask the question: How does the Bible's identification of these three affect the way you worship?

How about now, after all we have studied? Check each response of worship that you believe has been strengthened within you as a result of your study.

_____ Awe	_____ Enlightenment	_____ Joy
_____ Commitment	_____ Expectation	_____ Love
_____ Confidence	_____ Gratitude	_____ Mystery

How would you describe the doctrine of the Trinity to a friend?

Think

📚 To Learn More

Grace, Faith and Holiness by H. Ray Dunning

A Wesleyan-Holiness Theology by J. Kenneth Grider

Christian Theology (three volumes) by H. Orton Wiley

We Hold These Truths by Earle Wilson

All additional books and resources are available from Wesleyan Publishing House at www.wesleyan.org/wph or by calling 800.4.WESLEY (800.493.7539).

Notes

1. Adapted from Bruce L. Shelley, *Church History in Plain Language* (Dallas: Word Publishing, 1995), 115.
2. The author of this section is indebted to J. Kenneth Grider and Thomas C. Oden, *A Wesleyan-Holiness Theology* (Kansas City, Mo.: Beacon Hill Press of Kansas City), 158–159.

Personal Spiritual Journal

DATE _____

_____

_____

_____

_____

_____

_____

_____

_____

_____

_____

_____

_____

_____

My Prayer Today—

_____

_____

_____

_____

CHAPTER 5

Knowing God Through His Story

Christian History

> *"On this rock I will build my church, and the gates of Hades will not overcome it."*
>
> —Matthew 16:18

 **Bible Basics**

Matthew 16:13–19

[13]When Jesus came to the region of Caesarea Philippi, he asked his disciples, "Who do people say the Son of Man is?" [14]They replied, "Some say John the Baptist; others say Elijah; and still others, Jeremiah or one of the prophets." [15]"But what about you?" he asked. "Who do you say I am?" [16]Simon Peter answered, "You are the Christ, the Son of the living God." [17]Jesus replied, "Blessed are you, Simon, son of Jonah, for this was not revealed to you by man, but by my Father in heaven. [18]And I tell you that you are Peter, and on this rock I will build my church, and the gates of Hades will not overcome it. [19]I will give you the keys of the kingdom of heaven; whatever you bind on earth will be bound in heaven, and whatever you loose on earth will be loosed in heaven."

Connecting God's Word to Life

The church is built upon Jesus, the Son of God. In what ways is your life built upon the life and teaching of Jesus?

The Formation of the Church (A.D. 30–500)

The sign on the front of the church read "Founded A.D. 30." Obviously this local church wasn't claiming to be that old, but they were linking themselves to the event which launched the church soon after the death, resurrection, and ascension of Christ.

If they were making a statement about their roots, they were right. The Day of Pentecost was the birthday of the Christian church. Although precise dates are sometimes difficult to determine in the biblical period, that historic event happened around the year 30 A.D. The book of Acts, chapter 2, tells us that three thousand charter members joined the church as a result of the awesome outpouring of God's power on that day, and, as the saying goes, the rest is history. God's redemptive plan had begun in the Old Testament, of course, and reached a crescendo in the story of Jesus. But for the body of believers called *the church*, Pentecost was Day One.

Perhaps, though, the "A.D. 30" sign was meant to imply something else. Perhaps they were saying that their modern congregation had an immediate and direct connection to the New Testament church. Maybe they thought they could leapfrog backwards over history without acquiring any debt to or legacy from the generations of Christians in the two thousand years between the Day of Pentecost and the day they opened their church doors. If that's what they meant, they're mistaken. God moves through history and He certainly moves through the history of His church. If the church is the family of God, then its history is our family tree.

The book of Acts was the earliest book of church history. This book, penned by Luke, traced the spread of the early church "in Jerusalem, and in all Judea and Samaria, and to the ends of the earth" (Acts 1:8). Luke recorded the early efforts of apostles and many unknown disciples of Christ who were effective early missionaries and evangelists. By the middle of the book, his focus shifted to follow the missionary journeys of Paul and especially his remarkable success after the Jerusalem Conference (Acts 15) opened the door to the evangelization of Gentiles, or non-Jews.

> *The blood of the martyrs is seed.*
>
> —Tertullian
> A.D. 200

As the church spread, the believers who were now called Christians (Acts 11:26) faced both external and internal challenges. Their main external problem was persecution. First the Jewish religious leaders and then Roman government officials attacked the new church. Stephen (Acts 7) proved to be the first in a long and honored line of Christians who would die for their faith. Yet the hotter the fires of persecution burned, the stronger the church became. The growth of the persecuted church was phenomenal. Tertullian, an early Christian leader wrote, "The blood of the martyrs is seed." Four major, empire-wide efforts and countless regional campaigns failed to destroy Christianity. A new day dawned for the church when the Roman Emperor Constantine became a Christian and declared Christianity a legal religion in 313. Now favored by Rome, the church expanded even more rapidly across the empire.

Internally, the church faced the problem of heresy. In those formative years, some taught error instead of truth—wrong ideas about Christ, the Trinity, the Bible, sin, or any of a hundred other doctrinal issues. Paul (1 Tim. 1:3), Peter (2 Pet. 2:1), and John (1 Jn. 4:1) all warned against false teachers in the New Testament church, but false teachers abounded. The Gnostics, for example, called themselves Christians but linked salvation to a secret knowledge that they believed they had, of course. They argued for the existence of not one but two gods, one of them good and the other evil. Another group, the Ebionites, insisted that Jesus was the human son of Joseph and Mary who was "adopted" by God at His baptism. As time passed, the church responded to these heresies in three ways. Under the direction of the Holy Spirit, the church leadership gradually settled on twenty-seven inspired books to include in the New Testament canon. They utilized simple baptismal creeds as approved statements of belief, and they gave increased authority to their ministerial leaders to deal firmly with those who spread misinformation and created discord. Another avenue of orthodoxy (right beliefs) became available after the conversion of Constantine. Church councils were convened to rule on matters of theology, such as the famous Council of Nicea (A.D. 325), which was the first ecumenical or worldwide council.

The stakes were high at Nicea. Arius, a popular bishop in Alexandria (Egypt), was teaching that Christ was a demi-god, less than God but more than a man. Athanasius opposed him and stood for the full deity and full humanity of Christ. When the council overwhelmingly rejected Arianism, the church cleared another hurdle placed in the path of truth. Athanasius, the hero of Nicea, is considered to be a pillar of the early church. He joined the company of such giants throughout church history as the writer and theologian Augustine, the Bible translator Jerome, the Christian apologist (defender of the faith) Justin Martyr, and St. Patrick, the missionary known by millions who know nothing else of church history.

The early church had been faithful through persecution and hardship, and by the grace of God they saw a new day arrive—a day of peace, prosperity, and even power and influence with the secular authorities. But was that change healthy? Under persecution, the church had flourished spiritually. In power, the church would flounder.

In your opinion, is it easier to be a faithful Christian in the comfort and security of North America or in a country where Christians are physically persecuted? Why?

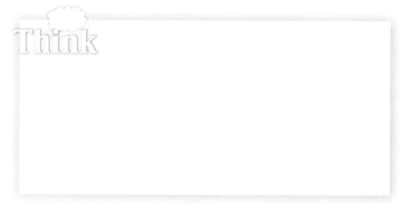

The Deformation of the Church (A.D. 500–1500)

It may seem negative to speak of "the deformation of the church" in the Middle Ages. Admittedly, it is not a standard phrase used in the study of church history. But the dictionary defines deformation as "distorted, warped, disfigured" and, unfortunately, that description fits this era.

There were a few bright spots, of course. Thomas á Kempis wrote *The Imitation of Christ* during this period, and he could well have written a sequel to illustrate it from the lives of medieval Christians who imitated Christ effectively. Thinkers like Anselm and William of Ockham anchored the faith intellectually at a time not known for its love of learning. Francis of Assisi and his co-worker, Clare, modeled self-denial to a church no longer known for denying itself much of anything. Raymond Lull gave his life as a pioneering missionary to the Muslin world.

Thomas á Kempis

Despite their faithful witness, though, the church seemed to lose its way. Doctrinal deviations arose, ethical standards lapsed, unity yielded to division, and the church which had honored Christ by shedding its blood for Him as He had shed His blood for it, began to shed the blood of others in His name.

The problems started at the top. Over time, the bishop of Rome had become more than a bishop. He had become a pope, officially claiming this preeminence by asserting that Peter had been the first pope. In reality, the rise of the papacy can be traced to several strong Roman bishops who held office after Christianity gained political and social influence. Under their leadership, the rule of the popes extended, at least theoretically, over the entire church and even over secular rulers. The church adjusted its organizational flow chart to say that, while Christ was the head of the church in heaven, the pope was the head of the church on earth.

Following the example of far too many popes, the cardinals and bishops of the church tended to build their own power bases, and the results were appalling—the buying and selling of church offices, the accumulation of great personal wealth, and sexual impurity among church leaders. Parish priests were another step down the ecclesiastical ladder, but they tended to view themselves as superior to the people they were supposed to serve. After all, didn't the priests speak the magical words that made Christ "appear" when the bread and wine were turned into the actual body and blood of Christ, as church theologians started teaching in the late 1100s? And didn't they recite the mass in Latin, a language no longer spoken by the vast majority of common folk? From the pope on his throne to the local priest on his pedestal, the clergy ruled the church.

Common Christians were left with what has been called *popular piety*, an elaborate system of less-than-biblical beliefs and practices which gave them the sense of participation in the faith that was so seriously lacking in public worship.

Superstitious people created a detailed mythology about Mary, the mother of Christ, exalting her to a place of importance just below the Trinity. The veneration of saints flourished and the calendar became filled to overflowing with saints' days. Christians were instructed to use saints as mediators of their prayers. Churches

Anselm

gathered various relics of the saints—their bones, their teeth, scraps of their clothing, strands of their hair, and promised spiritual blessings to those who made pilgrimages to view these relics.

The notion of purgatory also developed during this time. Never mind that there was no biblical basis for belief in an intermediate place after death in which the righteous must purge their souls by suffering in order to be worthy of heaven. The church taught it, so it must be so. The faithful were instructed to pray for the dead and purchase indulgences to free departed family members or friends from purgatory more quickly. All of these devotional practices kept common Christians coming to impressive churches and cathedrals that often towered over the landscape like the institutional church towered politically and socially over medieval society. However, the church of the Middle Ages was something less than a tower of moral, ethical, and biblical integrity.

The word *integrity* can also mean completeness or unity. In the eleventh century, the church lost that, too. Christianity around the world had up to this time been virtually a single church. To be a Christian was to be in *the* church, without denominational labels or independent branches of any significance. For that reason it was called the *catholic* church, which means worldwide or universal. (Even Christians who do not belong to the Roman Catholic Church still affirm the words of the Apostles' Creed, "I believe in the holy catholic church. . . .") In 1054, the eastern portion of the church split away and chose the name *Eastern Orthodox*. There were many points of conflict, but chief among them was the absolute authority of the pope. Today, Eastern Orthodox Christians total more than 250 million, mainly in the Greek Orthodox and Russian Orthodox churches.

Division in the church weakened it at a time when it needed all of its strength. A new rival had appeared outside the walls of the church, and those walls were badly battered by a force the world would come to know as *jihad*. By Mohammed's death in the year 632, Islam controlled all of the Arabian Peninsula. Within a generation it had spread across the Middle East, occupied portions of south central Asia, conquered North Africa, and even crossed the Mediterranean into Portugal and Spain before being driven back at the Battle of Tours in 732. Islam was expelled from Western Europe but eventually captured the historic Christian city of Constantinople (now Istanbul) in 1453, and expanded their influence into Eastern Europe.

During the Crusades, Christian Europe and Islam fought a series of wars for control of the Holy Land. Initial successes turned to ultimate failure for the armies of Christendom, and after two centuries of conflict (1095–1291), Christian holy sites remained under Muslim control. The status of Jerusalem and the Holy Land may not have changed, but something else had. The church had abandoned its spiritual weapons, listed in Eph. 6, for more traditional weapons of war. Having become accustomed to striking out against its foes in the

John Wycliffe

Middle East, the church used those same weapons to strike out against its enemies closer to home—and it defined enemies very loosely. One result was the Inquisition, a reign of terror that used torture to compel men and women to confess heresy.

Corruption. Greed. Coercion. It was not the church's finest hour, and we're tempted to hurry past these pages in the family album. But from within the church—and that's important to remember—from within the church God raised up some of the multitude who had kept the faith and set them to the task of recovering the values and vision which had been abandoned. In the 1300s, John Wycliffe called the church back to the Bible. A generation later John Huss died at the stake for daring to agree with Wycliffe. Their voices were largely ignored, but they set the stage for one who, by the grace of God, would be heard.

If the church is God's idea, how could it have gone so wrong so often? Since its past is far from perfect, how can we have hope for its future?

The Reformation of the Church (A.D. 1500–1700)

Indulgences are bad stewardship and worse theology. If souls can be freed from purgatory for money, why doesn't the church free them for nothing, out of Christian love? To say that the proceeds go to build St. Peter's Basilica in Rome is a weak argument; the pope is rich enough to build St. Peter's out of his own pocket. Indulgences are abuses, plain and simple, even though they are connected to the sacrament of penance. Christ calls us to repentance, not to penance. (*Ninety-Five Theses*, summarized)

It was this argument in an expanded form that Martin Luther nailed to the door of the Castle Church in Wittenberg, Germany, on October 31, 1517. Although no one suspected it at the time, least of all Luther, his Ninety-Five Theses were the opening shot in the struggle which led to the Protestant Reformation.

Martin Luther was a good Catholic. As a monk, he took his calling more seriously than did many around him. As a professor of Bible at the University of Wittenberg, he took the Scripture seriously, too. His study led him to Rom. 1:17—"The righteous will live by faith"—and it revolutionized his view of God, which in turn revolutionized his view of the church. His intent was not to attack the church but to reform it from within, and to that end he exposed one error after another.

At the core were three affirmations known as the Battle Cry of the Reformation: faith alone, Scripture alone, Christ alone. Faith alone is the door to salvation, not a combination of faith and good works. Scripture alone is our authority, not Scripture plus centuries of sometimes self-contradictory church tradition. Christ alone is the Head of the church, not Christ and the pope. To these principles Luther added others.

- Scripture supports two sacraments. Christ instituted only baptism and the Lord's Supper.

- The bread and wine do not literally become the body and blood of Christ.

- God's people have direct access to God. The priesthood of all believers means that we do not have to approach Him through a priest of the church.

- The Bible should be available in the language of the people, not just in a language (Latin) known only to priests and scholars. Worship should be conducted in the people's language as well.

- The reading and preaching of the Word, not the sacrament of the Lord's Supper, should be the primary focus of public worship.

- Congregational singing must be restored.

In 1521, Luther found himself in trouble not only with the pope but also with the emperor and the civil authorities. Since church and state were hopelessly intertwined, a challenge to the church was regarded as a challenge to the state. A legislative assembly known as a German diet met to consider his case in the city of Worms. Luther was charged with treason, and a guilty verdict would mean a death sentence. Offered a chance to repudiate his books and teachings, Luther refused and was declared an outlaw. He could be killed anywhere, anytime, by anyone, with the blessings of the state. He was certain his life was all but over.

He was wrong. Luther lived a full life with the support of the German people and under the protection of German princes who were strong enough to defy the emperor. He married and had a family, translated the Bible into German, wrote hymns like "A Mighty Fortress Is Our God" for his congregation to sing, and founded the body of believers known as the Lutheran Church.

Lutherans were the first Protestants, but they wouldn't be the last. The term *Protestant*, by the way, comes from a document of protest issued in the early days of the Reformation. Some felt that Luther had not gone far enough in his separation from the Roman Catholic Church. Ulrich Zwingli and John Calvin pushed for greater change. Their worship services featured little music, few symbols of the faith, and an even more reduced role for the Lord's Supper, all led by ministers who disdained the wearing of clergy robes. Advocates of this alternative form of Protestantism called it *Reformed*, implying that Luther wasn't reformed enough. Its more familiar label is Calvinism, after the man who did more than any other to establish it.

John Calvin left his study of law to create a holy commonwealth in Geneva, Switzerland, in which the church and the community would together be governed by the laws of God. His *Institutes of the Christian Religion* was the most influential theological work in Protestantism. In it he constructed an elaborate argument for predestination, the theological position which denies the free will of individuals and contends that God in His

Martin Luther

sovereignty chooses who will be saved and who will be lost. Christians who are descended from this branch of the Reformation still carry the name *Reformed*, as in the Christian Reformed Church and the Reformed Church in America. Calvin's theology has also shaped the views of Christians in other denominations such as Presbyterians and, to a lesser degree, Baptists.

A third branch of Protestantism was widely dismissed as the *Radical Reformation*. Anabaptists, or "re-baptizers," got their name because they rejected infant baptism and baptized (or re-baptized, according to their opponents) adults who had previously been baptized as infants. Actually, they stood for much more. They were among the first to call for separation of church and state, a congregational system of church government, and voluntary church membership in "free" churches. In addition, they lived by a high code of Christian discipline and morality, a characteristic that unfortunately was not shared by all Christians or even all Protestants. Based on Christ's command to turn the other cheek, Anabaptists were pacifists. They refused to fight, even in self-defense. It was a principle for which they would pay a high price. Because they were Protestants, Catholics targeted Anabaptists; because they were "radical," other Protestants also targeted them. As a result, they suffered tremendous persecution. The Mennonites, the Amish, and the Hutterites today represent Anabaptists. (Modern Baptists affirm their view of believer's baptism but do not actually trace their roots as a denomination back to the Anabaptists.)

It is from the fourth and final branch of the Reformation that most Protestants claim their heritage. For all the good that God has brought through the Church of England (or Anglican Church), its origin was anything but inspiring. Henry VIII of England was a strong Catholic king who had even been declared "Defender of the

John Calvin

Faith" by the pope in appreciation for his opposition to Luther. Yet Henry led his country into Protestantism merely for personal convenience, not because of any change in his religious views. Henry wanted a new wife. Katherine, his wife of eighteen years, had given him a daughter, Mary, but no son. Henry was determined to marry Anne Boleyn, a lady-in-waiting at the royal court, because he was convinced that she could produce a male heir. The pope denied his repeated requests for an annulment for political reasons. So Henry's advisors suggested a novel solution: create your own church, declare yourself its head, and grant yourself the annulment. He did just that, and the Church of England was born. Unfortunately for him (and even more unfortunately for Anne), she gave birth to another daughter, Elizabeth. Out of frustration he ordered Anne to be beheaded. His third wife, Jane Seymour, was the only one of his six wives who gave him the son he craved.

Branches of the Protestant Reformation
The Lutheran Church
The Reformed Churches
The Anabaptist Churches
The Church of England

Young Edward VI reigned as a Protestant, and his counselors saw to it that Protestantism became established in England. But he died at age fifteen and the throne passed to his Catholic sister Mary. Bent on restoring Catholicism, "Bloody Mary" sought to undo Edward's reforms by executing almost three hundred of the leading Protestants in England. When she died, her Protestant sister Elizabeth came to power, but those who expected the religious pendulum to swing once again to the opposite extreme were surprised by Elizabeth's precocious wisdom. She crafted a compromise: the Church of England would become barely Protestant. By her design it would look Catholic while remaining Protestant.

The Elizabethan Settlement was a diplomatic triumph. However, true Protestants in England felt that it left much to be desired. Those who urged Elizabeth to purify the church of all traces of Catholicism were called *Puritans*. They included several factions within the Church of England that would later become independent denominations— Presbyterians, Congregationalists, Baptists, and Quakers. Despite their differences, they were united against the compromise, but they found the queen immovable.

The Puritans didn't have any more success when they approached her successor, James I, with the same requests. However, at their urging, he authorized the project that created an English translation of the Bible known as the King James Version. Eventually the tensions between Puritans and royalists led to a civil war in England. The Puritans won that war and briefly ruled England under Oliver Cromwell. But when he died, the influence of Puritanism died with him. Puritans concluded that their best hope lay in the New World.

Protestantism had brought reformation. Some of the church's worst abuses had been eliminated, and some of its greatest ills had been remedied. Yet far too often the changes were more a matter of the head than the heart, especially after the first reforming generation passed from the scene. Reformation was not enough. The church needed revival.

The Protestant motto is Semper Reformandum—Always Reforming. Is it possible for the church to be "always reforming"? How?

The Transformation of the Church (A.D. 1700–Present)

If you had slipped into a worship service in a certain nominally Christian land three hundred years ago, you might have heard this prayer and praise report:

> The spiritual situation here just a few years ago was discouraging. God was honored in public and forgotten in private. You would have been hard pressed to find anyone who knew Him personally. Church attendance was abysmal, Christian education was practically non-existent, and few ministers of the church were warm-hearted believers themselves. Then, God stepped in and sent revival to us in . . .

Where? The answer is Germany. And England. And America! In perhaps the most remarkable era of spiritual renewal in history, God's Spirit moved in three strategic countries in quick succession.

The German revival began in the Pietist Movement led by Philip Jacob Spener. Lutheranism was theologically sound but spiritually cold, and Spener lit a fire under Germany's national church with his emphasis on the new birth. Through home Bible studies and prayer meetings, Pietism spread across Germany and into nearby Holland and Scandinavia. The University of Halle became its educational center, and from its graduates came some of Protestantism's earliest foreign missionaries. Count Nicholas von Zinzendorf, a Lutheran Pietist in Germany who became the leader of a dynamic refugee church called the Moravians also sent out missionaries.

It was a Moravian missionary who led John and Charles Wesley to an experience of saving faith. The Wesley brothers were sons of an Anglican minister and his wife,

Samuel and Susanna Wesley, and grew up in the quiet English village of Epworth. After five-year-old John was rescued at the last possible moment from the fire which destroyed their parsonage, Susanna was convinced that God had great plans for this "brand plucked from the burning" and resolved to raise him with that in mind. While John was teaching at Oxford and Charles was a student there, they started a campus group that other students mocked as "the Holy Club." These young *Methodists* (another slur which they would later adopt as their name) worked hard at being Christians, and the Wesleys even came to the new American colony of Georgia to spread the gospel. They returned to England

John Wesley   Charles Wesley

disappointed and disillusioned. Something was missing. A Moravian by the name of Peter Boehler convinced them both to trust in Christ rather than their good works for their salvation. The brothers testified to a life-changing experience of God's grace within days of each other. For John, it happened at a religious society meeting, patterned after the model of the Pietist home devotional meetings, on Aldersgate Street in London on May 24, 1738.

Soon he discovered his life's ministry. For fifty years he traveled across England, preaching in the open air and organizing his converts into Methodist societies. He also became one of England's greatest Christian social reformers, working to improve the lot of the poor, alleviate the horrible conditions in English prisons, and end slavery in the British Empire. Wesley is seldom given credit as a theologian, but he recovered for the church several scriptural truths that had slipped into obscurity: holiness of heart and life, or "perfect love;" assurance of salvation; and free will (as opposed to predestination). Charles Wesley's primary contribution to the revival was his incredible output of more than six thousand hymns, among them many of the greatest hymns in the English language. Together the brothers were the catalysts for the Wesleyan Revival, which had a profound impact not only on Great Britain but also on America, through the Methodists who brought their faith to the colonies.

When those Methodists arrived in the American colonies, they found a national revival already in progress called the Great Awakening. By the 1730s and 1740s, God had begun to move on the hearts of ministers and laity alike in churches from Pennsylvania to Massachusetts. The one whom He chose to fan those sparks into a blaze was an English evangelist named George Whitefield, a friend of the Wesleys and a fellow member of the Holy Club. Whitefield, who

George Whitefield

communicated biblical truth with a dramatic flair in the pulpit, made seven trips to America. The revival he helped to establish lasted off and on for forty years, and by the time it ended in the 1770s, fifty thousand people had been converted. Historians have stated that the Great Awakening did more to unite the thirteen original colonies than did anything else in the days leading up to the American Revolution. "One nation, under God" was a fact long before that phrase found its way into the pledge of allegiance.

Amazingly, a Second Great Awakening soon followed the first. Through campus revivals in the East and a new phenomenon out West called the *camp meeting*, people turned to God in the years after the Revolutionary War just as they had in the years preceding it. The "new measures" of lawyer-turned-evangelist Charles Finney revolutionized revivalism. His "protracted meetings" provided the model for what would become local church revival meetings, and his "anxious bench" for seekers led to today's altar call. Finney had his critics. In fact, both the first and second awakenings were opposed by some in the religious establishment. But, like the Pietist Movement in Germany and the Wesleyan Revival in England, they transformed the church and, to a great degree, the nation.

In general, it was the theologically liberal wing of the church that discounted religious revivals. They believed that truth was to be found in human reason more than in God's revelation. As this position gained cultural acceptance in America, many of the largest denominations became increasingly liberal, at least in terms of their leadership. On the other hand, evangelical Christians (*evangelical* coming from the New Testament word meaning "gospel") still championed "the faith that was once for all entrusted to the saints" (Jude 3). They affirmed the authority of the Bible, the necessity of the new birth, and the importance of evangelism—the same transforming message preached in the great revivals.

Within the ranks of evangelicalism was a family of churches that took transformation one step further. The Holiness Movement proclaimed the transforming power of the Holy Spirit in the experience of entire sanctification. That's what Wesley preached, and until 150 years ago it was a central theme in the

Methodist message. When Methodism cooled on the doctrine, its supporters withdrew from (or were pushed out of) Methodism and formed separate denominations, linked to each other by their commitment to preach and teach holiness. To the degree that they do so, the Wesleyan Revival continues today.

Charles Finney

The twentieth century has seen a number of other significant developments in Christian history. The faith is expanding at an unprecedented rate in Africa, South America, and parts of the Far East. Pentecostalism is now the world's fastest-growing major religious movement. Roman Catholicism reinvented itself in many ways in the momentous Vatican II conference of the 1960s, and the implications of that directional shift are still being worked out. Liberal denominations are in statistical decline. Only God knows the future of these and other trends.

One thing we can know. Christ built His church on the rock of Peter's confession, and nothing in this world or the next will overcome it.

In what ways can a transformed church transform its world?

An Outline of Church History
The Formation of the Church (A.D. 30–500)
The Deformation of the Church (500–1500)
The Reformation of the Church (1500–1700)
The Transformation of the Church (1700–Present)

To Learn More

Christian History Magazine, published by Christianity Today

Christianity Through the Centuries by Earle E. Cairns

Church History in Plain Language by Bruce Shelley

Here I Stand: A Life of Martin Luther by Roland Bainton

A Real Christian: The Life of John Wesley by Kenneth J. Collins

All additional books and resources are available from Wesleyan Publishing House at www.wesleyan.org/wph or by calling 800.4.WESLEY (800.493.7539).

Turning Points in Church History

A.D. 30   Pentecost: The Birthday of the Church

49–50   Jerusalem Conference opens the door for evangelization of the Gentiles

313   End of persecution as Christian emperor Constantine assumes power

325   Council of Nicea affirms deity of Christ

367   New Testament canon is recognized in final form

432   Patrick goes to Ireland as a missionary

732   Battle of Tours stops advance of Islam in Western Europe

1054   The Great Schism results in separation of Eastern Orthodox Church from Roman Catholic Church

1095   First Crusade is launched

1206   Francis of Assisi begins life of poverty

1380   John Wycliffe oversees first translation of Bible into English (approximate date)

1415   John Huss is burned at the stake

1517   Martin Luther posts *Ninety-Five Theses*

1521   Luther takes stand at Diet of Worms

1525   Anabaptist Movement begins

1534   Henry VIII declares himself head of the Church of England

1536   John Calvin publishes *Institutes of the Christian Religion*

1620   Puritan Pilgrims land at Plymouth Rock

1675   Philip Jacob Spener founds Pietist Movement

1738   Aldersgate experience of John Wesley

1740   High-water mark of the Great Awakening

1830   Charles Finney's revivals begin in Second Great Awakening

1906   Azusa Street Revival introduces Pentecostalism

1943   C. S. Lewis publishes *Mere Christianity*

1948   Mother Teresa begins mission in Calcutta, India

1949   Billy Graham gains national visibility with Los Angeles Crusade

1962   Vatican II Conference gives Catholicism new approach and attitude

Personal Spiritual Journal

DATE _____

_____

_____

_____

_____

_____

_____

_____

_____

_____

_____

_____

_____

_____

_____

_____

_____

My Prayer Today—

_____

_____

_____

_____

CHAPTER 6

What Christians Believe

Doctrine

Watch your life and doctrine closely. Persevere in them, because if you do, you will save both yourself and your hearers.

—1 Timothy 4:16

 **Bible Basics**

1 Timothy 4:7–16

⁷Have nothing to do with godless myths and old wives' tales; rather, train yourself to be godly. ⁸For physical training is of some value, but godliness has value for all things, holding promise for both the present life and the life to come. ⁹This is a trustworthy saying that deserves full acceptance ¹⁰(and for this we labor and strive), that we have put our hope in the living God, who is the Savior of all men, and especially of those who believe. ¹¹Command and teach these things. ¹²Don't let anyone look down on you because you are young, but set an example for the believers in speech, in life, in love, in faith and in purity. ¹³Until I come, devote yourself to the public reading of Scripture, to preaching and to teaching. ¹⁴Do not neglect your gift, which was given you through a prophetic message when the body of elders laid their hands on you. ¹⁵Be diligent in these matters; give yourself wholly to them, so that everyone may see your progress. ¹⁶Watch your life and doctrine closely. Persevere in them, because if you do, you will save both yourself and your hearers.

2 Peter 3:18

> But grow in the grace and knowledge of our Lord and Savior Jesus Christ.
> To Him be glory both now and forever! Amen

 ## Connecting God's Word to Life

How do you know if what you believe is really the truth?

The Importance of a Biblical View

Mohammed Atta was an educated and devoted Muslim from one of the wealthiest nations in the Middle East. On September 11, 2001, he piloted the controls of an American Airlines jet as it crashed into one of the World Trade Center towers in New York City. His religious mentor promised him that for his efforts he would be welcomed into heaven's glory with a reward of seventy virgins.

On December 7, 1977, Eldon McCorkhill, 33, and Linda Cummings, 28, had a few drinks in a bar in Redlands, California, and talked about their beliefs in an after-life. Linda told her friend that she was firmly convinced of the reality of reincarnation. A spirited debate continued all the way back to McCorkhill's apartment. Once there, he pulled a loaded pistol out of his drawer and handed it to her. "If you believe in this, let's see what you'll come back as," he challenged. Linda took the gun, pointed it to her head and pulled the trigger.

In January 1956, the Auca Indians of Ecuador martyred Nate Saint, Jim Elliot, and three fellow missionaries. Nine years after this brutal slaying, the gospel of Mark was published in the Auca language. Among the many Aucas who turned to Christ were the six men who had killed the missionaries. Nate's sister, Rachel Saint, led the translation team used by God to reach the Aucas. She refused to shrink from the call of Christ to reach the very people who had brutally killed her brother.

What do these three stories have in common? They are stories of sincerely devoted people with deeply held, though widely divergent, beliefs, which led them to take specific, faith-led action steps. In dramatic fashion, they illustrate the truth that what we believe makes a difference! What we believe about the character of God and human nature—not to mention other theological topics—ultimately will shape our attitudes and actions. In the end, we all live out what we believe. If our beliefs are faulty, eventually those faulty beliefs will lead to faulty behavior. Knowing that, the Apostle Paul admonishes his young disciple, "Watch your life and doctrine closely . . ." (1 Tim.4: 16).

Beliefs ⇨ Behavior ⇨ Consequences

Unfortunately, many believers choose to neglect the study of the doctrines that undergird their faith. They believe, but their grasp of what they believe—not to mention why they believe it—remains sketchy at best. These believers are hard pressed to articulate a thoroughly biblical worldview or even core Christian beliefs.

The word *doctrine* sounds boring. Yet most people find that learning the foundational truths of the Christian faith is anything but boring. Upon discovering core biblical belief, new believers commonly respond with statements such as:

"I thought all religions believed basically the same thing. But now I see that biblical Christianity is truly unique."

"Theology and doctrine always seemed stale and boring. But now I see how relevant these beliefs are to my life."

"My faith has become so much stronger as I have grown in my understanding of what the Bible teaches."

Let's take a look at some key doctrines.

> What we believe about the character of God and human nature—not to mention other theological topics—ultimately will shape our attitudes and actions.

The Authority of the Bible

How do we know what is the truth? What is our measure or standard or authority? People have developed three basic answers to that question. Some people insist that we can never really know truth. Most others say that human reason is the final authority for testing our truth assertions. People who believe this are secular humanists. Unfortunately, human reason is limited, faulty, and changeable in response to new discoveries, fads, and cultural pressures.

The third and best alternative grows out of our faith that Almighty God has revealed truth to us and the Bible, God's Word, constitutes a written revelation to us. Indeed, the Bible claims this of itself. The Bible says, "All Scripture is God-breathed and is useful for teaching, rebuking, correcting and training in righteousness" (2 Tim. 3:16). Christianity claims that, while the Bible was written by men, those writers were so under the inspiration of God that what they wrote was not the wisdom of men but the Word of God. This revelation possesses an authority for faith and practice that surpasses human reason, church

God is the only one who can tell us what He is like.

tradition, or even human experience. This is not to say that reason, tradition, and experience are not vital to spirituality. They have their place, but the final authority for truth is God's revealed word that is found in the Bible.

It's not up to us to decide what God is like. God is the only one who can tell us what He is like and what He requires of us. He has revealed Himself to us through His Word, and we must align our beliefs about God with His revelation. Similarly with every aspect of doctrine, our faith is not merely the product of human reason, the church's teaching, or even our own experiences. We look to the Bible as our source for revealed truth and subject all other standards to the test of biblical authority.

But doesn't every religion have its own holy book? What makes the Bible a superior revelation to Islam's *Koran* or the Hindu *Vedas*? The full answer to this deserves much more space than we have here. But a study of comparative religions would reveal how uniquely the Bible is grounded in historical reality and how the answers it provides to the key questions of life ring true to the way life is and the way people are. Both the internal witness found within the Bible and the external witness found in history, archaeology, and other disciplines support the Bible's claim to be a "God-breathed" book.

So central is the Bible to the development of sound doctrine that John Wesley, who was a voracious reader, described himself as a "man of one book!" (To explore in depth this matter of the sufficiency and full authority of Scripture, look up these passages: Ps. 19:7; Matt. 5:17–19; Acts 17:2, 11; 2 Tim. 3:15–17; 2 Pet. 1:19–21; Rev. 22:8–19.)

Why is the Bible more reliable than opinion?

The Biblical View of God

Little Billy was busy with his crayons one afternoon. When his mother asked what he was drawing, Billy replied that he was drawing a picture of God. The mother thought for a moment and then informed her son, "But no one knows what God looks like." To which Billy quickly responded, "They will when I'm finished!"

While it is true that God is a spirit who cannot be reduced to a picture form, the Bible paints a remarkable picture of the nature and character of the one, true, and living God. Among His many attributes are those that reflect the infinite side of His being. He is eternal, unlimited in power, wisdom, and goodness. He is the creator and preserver of all that exists (Gen. 1:1, Col. 1:16–17). There is a splendor, majesty, and glory to His being. He is a holy God, pure and perfect in every way.

Yet this infinite God is also intensely personal. He is a God of holy love. James 1:17 says, "Every good and perfect gift is from above, coming down from the father of the heavenly lights, who does not change like shifting shadows." Righteousness, justice, mercy, and grace make up the wonderful character of this God who relates to us as a heavenly father. The God of the Bible is pictured as the sovereign ruler of the universe.

Unique to this biblical view of God is the trinity or tri-unity of His being—one God who exists in three Persons. This eternal community of holy love at the center of the Godhead is one of the great mysteries. The Bible consistently affirms that there is one living and true God (Deut. 6:4). Yet, according to the same Bible, the Father is God, Jesus Christ the Son is God, and the Holy Spirit is God.

The clearest and most personal revelation God has given us of Himself came with the incarnation of God in the person of Jesus Christ. While Jesus was fully man, He was also fully God. His life, from its conception by the Holy Spirit and His virgin birth, to the miracles He performed and the sinless life He lived, to His sacrificial death on a cross and His triumphant resurrection from the dead and ascension into Heaven, gives evidence that He is the Divine Messiah.

God continues to work in our world through the ongoing ministry of the Holy Spirit. Of the same essential nature, majesty, and glory as the Father and the Son, the Holy Spirit administers God's grace to us. His ministry includes awakening, convicting, regenerating, sanctifying, assuring, preserving, guiding, and enabling those who respond in faith.

This biblical view of God is radically different from that found in other religions. Compared to the pantheism of Hinduism or even the portrait of Allah found in the Islamic *Koran*, the God of the Bible is unique and marvelous. We can only stand in amazement at the glory of this God who is both infinitely beyond us and yet intensely personal toward us.

What is the role of each member of the Trinity? Pause to worship God and to thank Him for revealing Himself to you.

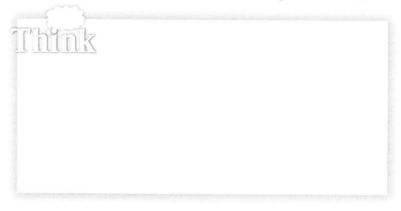

The Biblical View of Humanity

A faith that is true must account for both the wonder and the wickedness of human beings. According to Gen. 1:27, human beings were created in the image of God to enjoy a love relationship with Him and with their fellow image-bearers. Everything that is good about us—from the capabilities of the human mind to the kindnesses we show to others—can be traced back to the image of God within us. God created us to live in community with Him in a relationship of mutual knowing, loving, serving, and celebrating. Similarly, God created us to live in community with one another, where we can know and be known, love and be loved, serve and be served, and celebrate and be celebrated.

As His image bearers, we are endowed with the capacity to make moral choices.

Both the Bible and secular history record the story of the rebellion of the human race against the will of God. The Bible defines sin as both actions that violate the law of God and a condition that has corrupted human nature. We are born into this world with a sinful nature that accounts for the inclination toward evil that plagues us all. We are not good or godly by nature. As a result, we fall short of the glory of a holy God (Rom. 3:23). Our sin not only wreaks havoc in our relationships with one another; it also makes us deserving of the righteous judgment of God. We are spiritually dead and in desperate need of salvation.

In many ways the Bible gives us both good news and bad news about humanity. It is good news to discover that we are created in the image of God and thus all human life possesses dignity, value, and remarkable capacity. But our moral depravity is bad news. Our condition is hopeless apart from God's intervention. Someone has said that the gospel is bad news before it can become good news. The good news is that God in His great mercy and love has not left us to ourselves. John Wesley coined the term *prevenient grace* to describe the grace of God that is bestowed freely upon all people, enabling all that will to turn and be saved.

What great purposes provide meaning for your life?

The Biblical View of Salvation

Little Chris was having a tough time with math. Nothing Mom or Dad tried seemed to help. Out of desperation they enrolled Chris in a Catholic school known for its academic discipline. Everyday Chris came home from school, marched up to his room, and hit the books. He came down from supper, ate quickly, and promptly returned to his studies. Day after day, Chris followed the same regimen. Report card time rolled around and Chris came home, dropped his report card on the table and went up to his room to study. When Mom opened the card she was thrilled to see an

"A" in math. She went up to Chris' room and began to question her son, "What made the difference, Chris? Was it the nuns? Was it the books?" Chris shook his head, "No. If you must know, Mom, on that first day of class when I walked into the room and looked up on the wall and saw that guy nailed to the plus sign, I knew they didn't mess around in this school!"

Poor Chris had a lot to learn about "that guy nailed to the plus sign." At the center of the Christian gospel is the work that Jesus Christ accomplished when He laid down His life on the cross. The cross has become the most visible symbol of the Christian faith because it plays a central role in God's great plan of salvation. That plan had to solve the grand dilemma of how a sinful race, lost and helpless, could be reconciled to a holy God. The answer to that dilemma could not come from any mere human. But at the cross, God found a way to release His gracious forgiveness and pardon in a way that did not violate His holiness, righteousness, and justice (see Rom. 3:24–26). Christ offered Himself as the perfect sacrifice for the sins of the world, making His perfect righteousness available to humanity.

Many people stumble over the Bible's insistence that "there is no other name under heaven given to men by which we must be saved" (Acts 4:12). But the reality is this: apart from the grace of God that offered up Christ as a sacrificial atonement for sin, there is no hope for our salvation. Salvation is not something we can earn by our good works or our religious practices. Salvation is a gift of God's grace.

We gain access to this grace through faith (see Eph. 2:8 and Rom. 5:1–2). Saving faith is an important, but often misunderstood, responsibility that God has placed before every person. It is not merely an intellectual conviction. James 2:19 tells us that even demons believe that there is one God, but that intellectual assent does not save them. Saving faith leads us to repent by turning away from sin and sinfulness, and turning to Jesus Christ by receiving Him as Savior and Lord.

> Salvation is not something we can earn. It is a gift of God's Grace.

Several things happen when we take this step of repentance and faith. Here is a list of some of the great theological terms associated with our salvation:

Justification is a judicial term that involves the pardon of sin and the establishment of a righteous relationship with the holy God (Acts 13:38–39; Rom. 1:16–17; Phil. 3:9).

Regeneration is the work of the Holy Spirit that creates new spiritual life in people who have been dead in sin (John 3:3–8; 2 Cor. 5:17; Eph. 2:4–5).

Adoption signifies that someone who was outside the family of God has been adopted as a child of God (Rom. 8:14–15; Gal. 4:5–7)

Assurance is the work of the Holy Spirit now residing within us that witnesses to our spirit that we children of God (Rom. 8:16).

These precious gifts belong to people who cross the line of faith and become followers of Jesus Christ. Thus begins the great adventure of living the spiritual life.

Why is faith in Jesus the only way to be saved?

The Biblical View of the Spiritual Life

Coming to Christ marks the beginning of a new life "in the Spirit" (Rom. 8:9; Gal. 5:16). It is important to remember that our good works are *not* the basis of our salvation. We are saved by grace, not our own good works. But the person who is saved now finds that saving faith leads to a new desire and an ability to do the good works that God created His people to perform (Eph. 2:10).

This is not to say that we live perfectly sinless lives. The reality is that the same free will that was exercised in sinful ways prior to coming to Christ can still be exercised in sinful ways after our conversion. The Bible warns us to guard our life because in this fallen world, it will always be possible to fall into sinful patterns that can wreak devastating consequences in our lives. When we do sin, the Holy Spirit within us will prompt us to confession, forgiveness, and restoration (1 John 1:8–9). However, it is our responsibility to choose to respond submissively to His prompting.

The work of the Holy Spirit in the believer goes beyond the conviction of sin. God's desire is to set us free from the power of sin so we can live in full harmony with the perfect love of God. This work of the Spirit is called *sanctification*, which refers to the process God uses to transform our sinful character into conformity with His holy character (Heb. 13:12; 1 Pet. 1:15). The goal of this process is to make us like Christ in our character and conduct. All the resources of the Kingdom are now available to make holiness both an attainable goal and a present possibility for every believer.

The work of sanctification in a believer goes through several stages.

Initial sanctification begins at the moment we give our lives to Christ. Every true believer receives the precious gift of the indwelling Holy Spirit. This initial sanctification leads to a gradual process of spiritual growth in grace. During these early stages of growth, we experience both the joys of the Spirit's influence as well as the internal conflict with our sinful nature and residual pre-Christian habits. The inconsistency of this internal conflict, compounded by the ongoing influence of the world, the flesh, and the Devil, can often discourage us. We grow tired of living in part-time victory and spiritual weakness.

As we read the New Testament, we discover a resounding call to continue to grow in the process of sanctification, but we also find a call to a deeper consecration. Rom. 12:1 urges Christians to "offer your bodies as living sacrifices, holy and pleasing to God." This process of sanctification leads to the crisis moment when we consecrate our lives completely to God. Wesley and his followers called this experience *entire sanctification*. What is most significant about the experience of entire sanctification is the work that the Holy Spirit does in response to our act of consecration. This work involves a deep cleansing of the totally yielded heart, a deep infusion of the perfect love of God, and a deep empowering for holy living and effective service.

> This process leads to a moment when we consecrate our lives completely to God.

Some have misconstrued the idea of entire sanctification to mean a life without the possibility of sin. While such a state would be wonderful, Wesley recognized that we still live out our lives in a fallen world. While we may live without willfully disobeying the known will of God, we will always be subject to temptation and will continue to struggle with our infirmities and weaknesses. Still, the Holy Spirit enables us to grow in obedience to God's will and to produce the fruit of the Spirit in our lives (Gal. 5:22–23). Spiritual growth continues even after entire sanctification, making holiness a lifelong experience.

In addition to His work of sanctification, the Holy Spirit gives spiritual gifts to help us to live the spiritual life. Actually, the preeminent gift of the Spirit is the Holy Spirit Himself. He also gives each believer spiritual abilities that uniquely equip us for effective service as members of the Body of Christ. The most comprehensive lists of these spiritual gifts are found in Rom. 12 and 1 Cor. 12. The discovery, development, and deployment of our spiritual gifts help us to find our niche in the ministry of the church and can become a source of deep fulfillment and fruitfulness in the spiritual life.

What deeper work do you sense the Holy Spirit desiring to do in you?

The Biblical View of the Church

On the way home from church one Sunday, the Miller family began critiquing the Sunday service. Dad thought the preacher preached too long; Mom noted that the choir was off key; Sally complained about the big hat worn by the lady in the front pew. Finally, Mikey looked at Dad and winked, "I thought it was a pretty good show for a nickel!"

Is that all that church is—a pretty good show for a nickel? A biblical view of the church has little to do with the buildings, services, worship styles, or committees of a particular congregation. Local churches are a visible manifestation of the church, which is composed of everyone that believes in Jesus Christ and acknowledges Him as the founder and Head of the church. The mission of the church is to carry on the work of Christ until He returns; that work includes evangelism, discipleship, fellowship, and worship. These biblical purposes should shape the priorities of each local church.

It is not enough to make a profession of faith in Christ. The New Testament clearly indicated that as people came to Christ, they were immediately enfolded into a local body of believers. Down through history God has raised up a variety of churches and movements to fulfill the biblical purposes of the church and to reach the variety of people who need Christ.

Most Protestant churches believe that Christ ordained water baptism and the Lord's Supper as a sacramental means of grace to those who participate by faith. In the Lord's Supper we are reminded of the death of Christ and the renewal of the life, which can only be found in His grace. Likewise, baptism is an outward sign of an inward work of grace. By this step of obedience, new believers declare their faith in Christ.

What does it take for a church to become a biblically functioning community?

The Biblical View of Last Things

Mary came down from her bedroom and asked her mother, "Is it true that we came from dust?" "Yes," Mother replied. "And is it true that when we die, we return to dust?" Again Mother replied, "Yes. But why do you ask, honey?" Mary explained, "Well, I just looked under my bed and there's a whole bunch of people either coming or going!"

The question of where we are going and what the future holds is an important part of our theology. The Bible sends some very clear signals regarding the way this world will come to an end. First and foremost, Christ promised that He would make a personal return to earth to mark the end of this age (Matt. 16:27; John 14:3; Acts 1:11). His coming would signal the final and complete triumph over evil (Rev. 19:11–21). This coming would be followed by the resurrection of the dead and the judgment of humanity (Rev. 20:5–14).

A biblical worldview affirms that there is an eternal destiny awaiting us all. The Bible paints a glorious picture of heaven as a place of blessedness for all those who choose the salvation that God provides through Jesus Christ. Likewise, the Bible paints an agonizing picture of hell as a place of everlasting misery and separation from God for all who reject this great salvation.

We are to live in the light of these eternal realities. Our hope is this. We don't just live for today because our destiny is the incredible Kingdom that belongs to our holy God. This hope spurs us on to live holy lives and to reach out to a lost and dying world. We would be most foolish to face eternity without a Savior and to sacrifice the glory of heaven for the cares and trinkets of this world. We live every day between these two eternal destinies.

Lifelong Learning

This chapter has been a brief summary of basic Christian beliefs. Don't stop there. Go further. Dig deeper. Build your theology on the firm foundation of God's Word. As the Apostle Paul says, "Watch your life and doctrine closely." What we believe really does make a difference!

How would your behavior change if you knew that Jesus would return today?

To Learn More

Beliefs That Matter Most by W. T. Purkiser

Common Ground edited by Everett Leadingham

I Believe: Now Tell Me Why edited by Everett Leadingham

We Hold These Truths by Earle Wilson

All additional books and resources are available from Wesleyan Publishing House at www.wesleyan.org/wph or by calling 800.4.WESLEY (800.493.7539).

Personal Spiritual Journal

DATE _____

_____

_____

_____

_____

_____

_____

_____

_____

_____

_____

_____

_____

_____

_____

My Prayer Today—

_____

_____

_____

_____

CHAPTER 7

Knowing Christ through His Word

Scripture

> *But seek first his kingdom and his righteousness, and all these things will be given to you as well.*
>
> —Matthew 6:33

 **Bible Basics**

Matthew 5:17–20

[17]"Do not think that I have come to abolish the Law or the Prophets; I have not come to abolish them but to fulfill them. [18]I tell you the truth, until heaven and earth disappear, not the smallest letter, not the least stroke of a pen, will by any means disappear from the Law until everything is accomplished. [19]Anyone who breaks one of the least of these commandments and teaches others to do the same will be called least in the kingdom of heaven, but whoever practices and teaches these commands will be called great in the kingdom of heaven. [20]For I tell you that unless your righteousness surpasses that of the Pharisees and the teachers of the law, you will certainly not enter the kingdom of heaven."

 Connecting God's Word to Life

We know that salvation doesn't depend on own good works. Yet the Pharisees were known for doing "all the right things." What do you think Jesus meant when He said that our righteousness must surpass theirs?

Extreme Righteousness

The Pharisees were the religious elite of Jesus' day. If you had been living in the first century A.D., no doubt you would have greatly revered the Pharisees for their piety and scrupulous attention to the Law. This religious group was so concerned about meticulously keeping the Ten Commandments and the other laws God gave to Moses (see Exod. 20–23) that they came up with their own set of rules to govern every aspect of their daily lives. Their intent was admirable: they wanted to fully obey God. But something was missing. Jesus often condemned the Pharisees for their hypocrisy. They were following a list of rules but in the process forgot about love, justice, and compassion. They substituted outward righteous actions for the inward righteousness God required.

But how does that apply to us? Jesus said in order to enter the kingdom of heaven our righteousness must surpass that of the Pharisees. Let's look at three key passages in the Bible that teach us about the righteousness God requires: the Ten Commandments, found in Exodus, chapter 20, the Great Commandments found in Matt. 22:34–43, and the Sermon on the Mount, found in Matthew, chapters 5–7.

The Ten Commandments

Some 1200 to 1500 years before the time of Christ, God delivered His people (the Israelites) from bondage in Egypt through a series of plagues and by miraculously parting the Red Sea. He led them through the wilderness until they came to Mt. Sinai. There, on the top of the mountain, God met with Moses for forty days and gave him the Law—the Ten Commandments—along with many other regulations. These were not man-made laws; they were inscribed on tablets of stone by the finger of God Himself (Exod. 31:18). It was this Law that set Israel apart from all the other nations. It was a law based on God's holiness and righteous requirements.

The people in the other nations devised religions to appease their own lusts and appetites, often including debase sexual practices and drunken revelry. When people create their own religion, they devise a law that pleases them and that they can keep with little effort. But God's law was completely different. It was based on His character and highlighted our complete inability to fulfill it in our own power. God revealed Himself as holy and righteous, and He set forth for His people His expectations: They were to be holy and righteous because they belonged to Him.

The Ten Commandments are undoubtedly the most well known verses of the entire Bible. They're embraced as the essence of morality by Jews, Christians, and Muslims along with many other religious groups and governments. Quickly close your eyes. Can you name all ten of the commandments without peeking? If you can name five, you're doing better than most people. Complete the Commandment column of the following chart in your own words. (Save the other two columns for later.)

	Scripture	Commandment	Personal Struggle? Yes	No	Reveals Love for God	Others
1	Exod. 20:3		❏	❏	❏	❏
2	Exod. 20:4		❏	❏	❏	❏
3	Exod. 20:7		❏	❏	❏	❏
4	Exod. 20:8		❏	❏	❏	❏
5	Exod. 20:12		❏	❏	❏	❏
6	Exod. 20:13		❏	❏	❏	❏
7	Exod. 20:14		❏	❏	❏	❏
8	Exod. 20:15		❏	❏	❏	❏
9	Exod. 20:16		❏	❏	❏	❏
10	Exod. 20:17		❏	❏	❏	❏

No Other Gods

The Lord God demands that He hold first place in our lives. He must be our highest priority, with no other "gods" being placed ahead of Him in our devotion and allegiance. What are some modern-day gods that vie for our attention and affection?

No Idols

Not only does God require that He be honored above all gods, but He also demands that we rid ourselves of all idols that compete for our devotion. God didn't want His people to merely add Him to their list of deities and place Him on top. He expected them to worship Him and Him alone. After all, He is the only true God. Anything else is just a human-made mascot. Also, God didn't want them to make an earthly image of Him and to substitute human-made religion for a personal relationship with God.

> God doesn't want us to substitute human-made religion for a relationship with Him.

Honor God's Name

God's name was an expression of His character. It was to be revered. By tossing His name around casually, or by using it as an expletive, we profane it and show contempt for His holiness and uniqueness. Have you ever found yourself saying, "Oh, my God!" or "thank God!" when you really weren't thinking about God at all? If we're caught in the habit of casually using God's name as filler for conversation, how can we begin to break that habit?

Remember the Sabbath Day

God gave us a day of rest so we wouldn't get caught up in the affairs of the world. The Sabbath is His gift to us to rejuvenate our physical and mental resources and to refocus our minds on what's truly important in life. Read the following Scripture passages: Mark 2:23–28, Col. 2:16–17, and Rom. 14:5. How can we honor the Sabbath without making it a legalistic ritual?

Honor Your Father and Mother

This doesn't need much explanation, but it does require some reflection. Is there a difference between obeying our parents and honoring them? Is it possible to technically obey our parents and yet still dishonor them? Conversely, is it possible to honor our parents after we're grown without necessarily obeying their wishes?

Don't Murder

Don't intentionally and maliciously take another person's life.

Don't Commit Adultery

Any extra-marital sexual relationship is strictly forbidden in Scripture. Many Christians pride themselves on being pure in this regard, and yet they regularly sin by flirting with adultery. Read James 1:14–15. Where does sin begin? The outward act of adultery often begins when we fuel our desires by dwelling on impure thoughts, by dressing or acting suggestively, or by permitting exposure to pornography. How can we protect our hearts and minds from this destructive sin?

Don't Steal

This means not taking anything that doesn't belong to us. And we shouldn't conveniently forget to return something someone lent to us. This command doesn't just apply to material possessions. Don't steal someone's ideas, reputation, self-worth, or influence.

Don't Lie

Don't lie. Tell "the truth, the whole truth, and nothing but the truth." There's no room for "little white lies" or gossip in the life of a true follower of God. Deception can be a powerful temptation. While we may be technically truthful in our statements to others, we must be careful that the outcome isn't deception or slander. Even if we think our lie won't hurt anyone, it ultimately hurts our relationship with God.

> There's no room for "little white lies" or gossip in our lives.

Don't Covet

We shouldn't fervently desire what doesn't belong to us or occupy our minds with schemes of how to obtain possessions that belong to our neighbor. We must watch out if we are filled with jealousy over another's achievements or success (and plot to overthrow him or take the credit). If we put material possessions, prestige, or power above God—we are breaking the first commandment. In our materialistic society, how can we keep from constantly desiring the newest and best and from feeling deprived when we don't get it?

Return to the Ten Commandments chart. Indicate which commandments represent a personal struggle for you. Choose the one commandment you fear breaking. Write it below and list three specific actions you can do—or not do—to help you remain obedient.

Think

Commandment: _____

My Action Plan:

1. _____

2. _____

3. _____

The Greatest Commandment

One day a Pharisee, who was an expert in the Law, asked Jesus to name the greatest commandment in the Law. In Matt. 22:37–40, Jesus replied in this way. "'Love the Lord your God with all your heart and with all your soul and with all your mind.' This is the first and greatest commandment. And the second is like it: 'Love your neighbor as yourself.' All the Law and the Prophets hang on these two commandments."

Do you find these two listed in the Ten Commandments? The answer is, "Yes." Jesus said that the entire Law (and the Prophets) hinges on our love for God and our love for others. It is easy to become so focused on outward compliance with the Ten Commandments that we miss the inner foundation of love. The Pharisees certainly did, and they were supposed to be the experts! Read the story of the rich young man in Mark 10:17–22. He had been meticulous at keeping the commandments, but he lacked one thing, the foundation of love.

Most of us seem to either struggle with loving God or loving others. Either we instinctively love God and struggle to give proper love and concern for people, or we are so concerned with loving others that we fail to show proper love and respect for God. We need to examine our lives honestly before God. We'll never grow as disciples and become all that God wants us to be unless we honestly confront our sin and ask for forgiveness and for grace to live a life of balance.

Return to the Ten Commandments chart. In the remaining column, indicate whether obeying each commandment will demonstrate love for God or for others. Did you check both boxes for any of the ten? Why?

The Sermon on the Mount

Some people think there is no correlation between the Old Testament and the New, or they believe the New Testament makes the Old Testament obsolete. They couldn't be further from the truth! In Matt. 5:17, Jesus said, "Do not think that I have come to abolish the Law or the Prophets. I have not come to abolish them but to fulfill them." Jesus spoke these words in the context of the Sermon on the Mount, found in Matt. 5–7. In this memorable sermon delivered to His disciples near the Sea of Galilee, Jesus sets forth the ethical laws of the Kingdom He came to inaugurate. He shared God's requirements with them in a new and fresh way, which paralleled the Ten Commandments God had given them centuries before. He also addressed some of the Pharisees' 613 laws. Jesus came to fulfill the Law and to make it possible for us to live righteous lives by His power. He came to show us true righteousness (a righteousness that far exceeds that of the Pharisees). This is what God had expected all along.

Read the Sermon on the Mount, found in Matt. 5–7, noting especially the commandments from Exod. 20 that are amplified by Jesus. Use the following chart as a guide. (Note that Jesus didn't specifically mention all ten of the commandments, such as honoring your parents or keeping the Sabbath holy, but He did give guidelines that would apply to them.)

The Ten Commandments in the Sermon on the Mount	
1 No Other Gods	Matt. 6:24, 33, 7:21–23
2 No Idols	Matt. 5:3–10, 6:19–21, 31–32
3 Honor God's Name	Matt. 5:33–37, 6:7–9
4 Remember the Sabbath Day	Matt. 6:10–11, 25–34
5 Honor Your Father and Mother	Matt. 5:38–48, 6:14–15, 7:1–2, 9–12
6 Don't Murder	Matt. 5:21–26
7 Don't Commit Adultery	Matt. 5:27–32
8 Don't Steal	Matt. 5:30, 6:1–4, 28–33
9 Don't Lie	Matt. 5:33–37, 7:1–5
10 Don't Covet	Matt. 6:19–24

Jesus taught this sermon to His disciples. Disciples were learners, those who followed their master so closely—listening to his teachings, memorizing his words, copying his behavior—that they became virtual copies of the teacher. We, too, are called to be Jesus' disciples, not just casual or occasional followers. Let's look more closely at the Sermon on the Mount to see what we can learn about becoming more like Christ—about becoming true disciples. (The rest of this chapter will be more understandable if you first read the indicated passage from Matthew before reading the comments that follow.)

The Qualities of a Disciple: Matt. 5:3–12

This passage is known as the Beatitudes because of the repetition of the word "blessed." Here Jesus lists eight qualities that should characterize the life of a true disciple. They're not listed so we can pick and choose which ones we want to possess. We're expected to display all of them. As we seek to develop these qualities in our lives, Jesus says we will be blessed. To be blessed means to possess an inner happiness, contentment, and deep satisfaction. And it can only be achieved by cultivating these eight qualities.

Be Poor in Spirit. We do this by ridding ourselves of all pride and self-sufficiency. See Luke 18:9–14 for a good illustration. We must recognize that all our human righteousness is worthless and we are totally dependent on God's righteousness.

Be Mournful. Mourning is a passionate lament for a loved one, a sorrow that penetrates the soul. It implies great compassion for others (Rom. 12:15).

Be Gentle and Meek. The original term used here meant strength under control, calmness in the midst of pressure, or gracious courtesy. Think for a moment about Jesus' life because He was a perfect example of gentleness and meekness.

Notice the promise for those who are gentle: "They will inherit the earth." How different this is from the world's philosophy! The world believes meek people will be stepped on and end up last, but Jesus tells us we wind up the gainers, not the losers.

Be Spiritually Hungry and Thirsty. This is an insatiable appetite for righteousness, a passionate drive for justice, and the relentless pursuit of God. We tend to become complacent and satisfied with our own level of spirituality and to become apathetic toward sin and injustice in the world around us. But if we are true disciples, we will strive for holiness and righteousness both in ourselves and in our society. Our love for God and for others will compel us.

Did you notice the promise for those who hunger and thirst for righteousness? They will be filled or completely satisfied. The word used here for "filled" is the same word used to describe those who witnessed the miracle of the loaves and fish in Matt. 14. Jesus fed 5,000 men, plus women and children, with only five loaves of bread and two fish. Yet there were twelve basketfuls left over. It says in verse 20, "They all ate

> ## Jesus said that the meek are winners, not losers.

and were satisfied." That means they were completely full and content. God is always gracious to give us more of Him when we seek more of Him. If we draw near to God, He will always draw near to us.

Be Merciful. Mercy is active concern for those who are hurting. It is giving what is not deserved. It is getting personally involved and offering help. Pity is not enough; it takes effort. Read Matt. 25:31–46, 1 John 3:17, and James 2:15–16 for some ideas about how we can show mercy to others.

Be Pure in Heart. This refers to purity in our motives and intentions. It means there is no hatred, dissention, jealousy, or bitterness lurking in the recesses of our heart. Does this sound impossible? It is, without the grace and power of the Holy Spirit working in and through us.

The promise for those who are pure in heart is that "they will see God." Purity in heart (holiness) brings us close to His heart. Our eyes are opened so we can truly "see" Him, both now and for eternity.

Be a Peacemaker. This does not mean we should avoid conflicts or compromise our convictions to appease others. It is more than being merely relaxed or easy-going. Peacemakers are at peace with themselves and work to settle quarrels rather than to start or to advance them. Can you see why peacemakers are called "sons of God?" They stand out in the crowd and everyone recognizes they are godly. They work to restore broken relationships among others.

Be Glad in Persecution. The key to rejoicing in the midst of persecution is realizing that our reward is in heaven. We don't live each day for temporal, earthly reward or satisfaction, but for a reward that will last forever. Notice that these eight qualities don't lead to prosperity; they lead to blessedness. When we live the way God expects us to live, we will find a deep, abiding joy and contentment that is far greater than any material possessions or pleasures the world has to offer.

The deeper we grow in our commitment to becoming a true disciple of Christ, the more we will possess these qualities and desire the rewards Jesus mentioned. We are making progress when we find that we want God more than we want a new home or car. We are on the right track when we want to be called a child of God more than we want esteem from others. Then we will be the kind of Christians that God has called us to be and enables us to be.

Reasons for Joy

Link the quality praised in each beatitude with the promised reward.

Quality	Reward

As you read the descriptions of these beatitudes, which quality seems most lacking in your life? Name one practical thing you can do to cultivate that quality?

The Influence of a Disciple: Matt. 5:13-16

Jesus compared the influence of a true disciple to salt and light. Although salt is common today, it was so precious in Jesus' day that it was often given to soldiers as payment for wages. The phrase, "he isn't worth his salt," and our word *salary* comes from that practice. Think of how important salt was and still is. It enhances the flavor of everything it touches, but if we use too much it ruins our food. It preserves, heals, penetrates, melts ice, and creates thirst. Salt is no good if it stays in the shaker, and it should never draw attention to itself. True disciples are to act like salt in the world. As we stand for truth, our words and actions have a redeeming effect on the world around us. Our acts of compassion make the world a better, more livable place.

Our influence is also like light. Light exposes things that are hidden, illuminates our pathway, brings cheer, stimulates growth, and preserves life. Jesus said we shouldn't be secret Christians. We should let

> Jesus said we shouldn't be secret Christians. We should let our light shine

our light shine so others can benefit by coming in contact with our authentic, committed Christian example. We live lives that are different from those who don't know Christ. In addition to the verbal testimony that we give, our lives become shining examples of what God's love can do. That causes even nonbeleivers to praise God. In that way the "light" of our lives can lead others to acknowledge Christ.

How can you bless the people around you by being salt and light to them?

The Character of a Disciple: Matt. 5:17–48

Jesus taught that our righteousness must surpass the righteousness of the Pharisees in order for us to have eternal life. If we could simply follow a list of rules and make it to heaven, we wouldn't need Jesus at all. But think about it for a moment. Wouldn't it be a lot easier if we had a checklist to mark off every day? Read our Bible. Check. Pray before meals. Check. Go to church. Check. While those things are important, our character and our motives are of greatest concern. What Christ is doing *in* us is far more important than what we are doing *for* Christ. In this next section of the Sermon on the Mount, Jesus contrasted the Pharisees' external interpretation of the Law with the internal principles that should govern our lives as disciples. He gave six examples, each following the formula, "You have heard that it was said . . . But I tell you. . . ."

Obey from the Heart. Jesus cited two specific commandments: Do not murder and do not commit adultery. But He explained that it was love for others, not rules, that should govern our behavior. So He discussed the obvious corollaries: do not be angry and do not lust. We are not to allow anger to fester in us toward others or to belittle them. It's up to us to make amends if someone is angry toward us. We are responsible to make sure we're not causing someone else to sin, either by allowing them to remain angry at us or through divorce (see also Rom. 14:13–21).

Pursue Inward Integrity. Jesus said we should gouge out our eye or cut off our hand if it is causing us to sin. Surely Jesus didn't mean this literally! Or did He? He wants us to realize that God hates sin, and we must use drastic measures to deal with it (Habakkuk 1:13; Rom. 6:23; and Heb. 12:14). Knowing the consequences of our sin He urges us to pay any price to remain spotless. God has always demanded that

His people reflect His character. We're to be holy because He is holy.

Our integrity should be beyond reproach. Jesus used the example of keeping oaths to illustrate this point. The people of His day had developed an elaborate system of taking oaths. In fact, you had to swear by *something* for your word to be credible at all. It was a lot like when you were a kid and said, "Cross my heart and hope to die." It was proof that you were telling the truth. For true disciples, every word that comes from our mouths should be true and trustworthy. Our *yes* should always mean *yes* and our *no* should always mean *no*. People shouldn't have to second-guess us or to wonder if we're twisting our words to deceive. This is a matter of integrity and is an indication of what's in our hearts, for "from the overflow of the heart the mouth speaks" (James 3:2).

> Every word that comes from our mouths should be true and trustworthy.

Go the Extra Mile. Most people today are concerned about their rights, especially people who live in North America. We claim the right to be compensated if we're hurt, the right to live or work anywhere we want, to say anything we want, to do anything we want. We claim the right to be heard. True disciples understand that in Christ we have no rights. We give them all up to follow Jesus Christ, just as He gave up His rights when He was here on earth (the right to a fair trial, the right to respect). First Corinthians 6:19–20 tells us that we don't even belong to ourselves; we were bought at a price. Christ bought us through His shed blood on the cross. He owns us. We're His slaves. We don't have any rights.

> When God's love flows through us we can love others in a new way.

Jesus told us that as true disciples we should turn the other cheek, go the extra mile, love our enemies, and pray for those who persecute us. This goes against our very nature. And it all comes back to loving God and loving others. It's only when God's love flows through us that we are able to love others in a way that is unnatural to the rest of the world. We give up any right to vengeance or vindication. In our love, we become perfect, as our heavenly Father is perfect.

Is there something you need to cut out of your life in order to deepen your level of integrity as a disciple? What?

The Lifestyle of a Disciple: Matt. 6:1–18

Do you feel overwhelmed by the standard Jesus has called you to? Do you feel like it's impossible to live up to it? No doubt the disciples felt the same way! At this point they might have even been calculating how they were going to change or what they were going to start doing. Or maybe they were so overwhelmed they didn't know where to begin. So Jesus continues by explaining how to live the Christian life, warning about pitfalls and offering encouragement in the process.

Do Acts of Righteousness. Jesus began by warning against doing our acts of righteousness before people. He didn't say we're not to do them at all, because righteous acts are a natural result of a righteous heart. He listed three specific acts of righteousness we are expected to perform as disciples: giving to the needy, praying, and fasting (going without food for an extended period of time).

These good deeds are not ways to earn salvation or favor from God. But they are the overflow of our love for Him and for others and they should definitely be part of our lives. God expects us to do acts of righteousness.

Notice just a few of the instructions Jesus gave on prayer. It should be sincere and not just a routine repetition of words. We should pray for His will to be done on earth as well as praying for our daily needs. We shouldn't ask God to forgive us if we're not willing to forgive others.

Serve the God Who Sees in Secret. Although the Pharisees originally meant well, in time they became conceited about their spirituality. They did their righteous acts in a way calculated to attract public attention and honor to themselves. They wanted everyone to know how pious they were. But we shouldn't do that. Our motive in doing good should be to receive our answer and our reward from God, not people. Jesus pointed out that it is hypocritical to do good deeds without the proper motivation. We should always ask ourselves, "Who gets the credit?"

Expect Reward from God. Actually, the Pharisees all received a reward for their good works. They received exactly what they were looking for—acclaim from the people who observed them—but nothing more. When we do our acts of righteousness in secret with the proper motivation, we also receive a reward, one that is heavenly and spiritual. Don't be discouraged in living out the righteous life as a disciple. God will certainly bless us for putting our love for Him and our love for others into action.

Can you think of an act of kindness you could do for someone this week? Write it below, then do it without letting anyone know what you have done.

The Priorities of a Disciple: Matt. 6:19–34

When addressing priorities, Jesus spoke about money because, for many people, it is their prime motivation in life and their highest priority. In our capitalistic society most things revolve around money. Isn't money the primary determinant in many of our decisions? In this passage Jesus taught us that earthly treasures are fleeting. They can be lost in a moment. And in the end, they really don't satisfy the deepest longing of our hearts anyway. They are often just a substitute or a distraction from our real goals.

But we must be careful. Earthly riches or possessions can easily capture our affections. One of the most poignant principles in all of Scripture is this: "Where your treasure is, there your heart will be also" (Matt. 6:21). It's almost automatic. Think about it. When we spend a lot of money on a new car, we will love that car.

We'll take extra time to clean it and maintain it. If we devote a lot of time on a particular hobby, that, too, will capture our heart. It will be what we think about when we lie down at night and when we get up in the morning. Whatever we spend our greatest energy on will capture our heart. Wherever we place our "treasure" (and it's not always money), our heart is sure to follow. And, consequently, our devotion to God will be diminished. We can't serve two masters. Our highest priority should be Jesus and serving Him. That's what God stated in the first two of the Ten Commandments. Our love for Him must far exceed our love for anything else here on earth.

For most Christians, our preoccupation with money or earthly possessions has more to do with need than want. We're worried we won't be able to provide for our children or have the money to make ends meet. But we don't need to worry. Jesus promises that we are of great value to God (see also Matt. 10:30; John 3:16; and Matt. 6:8). He loves us and will always care for us, providing everything we need if our priorities are right. Whenever we seek God first and His righteousness, He takes care of everything else.

Describe an instance when God provided for you.

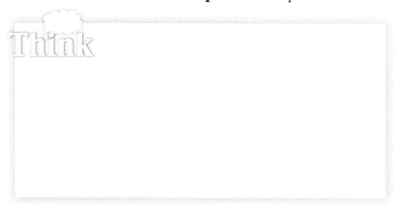

Guidelines for a Disciple: Matt. 7:1–29

Set Your Own Life in Order First. As we've worked through this chapter, we've probably thought of many applications to people we know: our husband or wife, parent, or maybe even our pastor. But every word of the Sermon on the Mount was written for us first. Jesus pointed this out to His listeners that day. He said we should correct our own big faults before we judge others and try to correct their little faults. We should continually meditate on God's Word asking God to show us what must be changed in our own lives.

Count on God's Supply. If we feel inadequate or defeated, remember that God will give us the righteous life we desire. All we have to do is ask, seek, and knock. God wants us to be righteous and holy even more than we want it. And He has the power to make it so. He wants to fill us with His love so we are able to love Him and others fully. But we have to want to first; we have to ask.

> God gave us the Ten Commandments, not the Ten Suggestions.

Enter at the Narrow Gate. We are responsible to choose the narrow road that Jesus has pointed out to us. Our goal shouldn't be to see how little we could do and still be considered disciples. We need to get as close to God as possible no matter whether anyone else joins us.

Choose Wisely Whom to Follow. False prophets abound. There are many people who will try to shipwreck our faith and lead us astray. Jesus described them as wolves in sheep's clothing. They may say and do all the right things, even performing miracles, but their fruit will always give them away. In Gal. 5:22–23 the fruit of the Spirit is described as: love, joy, peace, patience, kindness, goodness, faithfulness, gentleness, and self-control. We should be fruit inspectors before we take a bite! Is the person we want to follow obedient to the clear commands in God's Word? Are they doing the will of God?

Do you think Jesus has given us a lot of practical suggestions for growing in our spiritual life? He hasn't! Nothing He said in the Sermon on the Mount was a suggestion. God gave us the Ten Commandments, not the Ten Suggestions. Jesus knew that the only way to find true fulfillment, satisfaction, and contentment was by becoming true disciples. Blessings come to us when we put our Christianity into practice by living out the law of love.

At the end of the Sermon on the Mount, Matthew tells us that, "the crowds were amazed at his teaching, because he taught as one who had authority, and not as their teachers of the law." Jesus' words had authority, because He was speaking exactly what God told Him to speak (John 7:16; 14:10). You can purchase many books like this one that will help you grow in your Christian walk. But no other book can do for you what the Word of God can. His Word has authority and power. It will change your life.

What do you sense God telling you to do as a next step in becoming more like Jesus?

📚 To Learn More

Finding Your Maximum Happiness by Wilbur G. Williams

Discover the Word edited by Everett Leadingham

What Jesus Said About . . . edited by Everett Leadingham

Reflecting God Study Bible

All additional books and resources are available from Wesleyan Publishing House at www.wesleyan.org/wph or by calling 800.4.WESLEY (800.493.7539).

Personal Spiritual Journal

DATE _____

_____

_____

_____

_____

_____

_____

_____

_____

_____

_____

_____

_____

_____

My Prayer Today—

_____

_____

_____

_____

Scripture Index

Books of the Bible with Abbreviations

Old Testament

Genesis	Gen.
Exodus	Exod.
Leviticus	Lev.
Numbers	Num.
Deuteronomy	Deut.
Joshua	Josh.
Judges	Judg.
Ruth	Ruth
1 Samuel	1 Sam.
2 Samuel	2 Sam.
1 Kings	1 Kings
2 Kings	2 Kings
1 Chronicles	1 Chron.
2 Chronicles	2 Chron.
Ezra	Ezra
Nehemiah	Neh.
Esther	Esther
Job	Job
Psalms	Ps.
Proverbs	Prov.
Ecclesiastes	Eccles.
Song of Solomon	Song of Sol.
Isaiah	Isa.
Jeremiah	Jer.
Lamentations	Lam.
Ezekiel	Ezek.
Daniel	Dan.
Hosea	Hos.
Joel	Joel
Amos	Amos
Obadiah	Obad.
Jonah	Jon.
Micah	Mic.
Nahum	Nah.
Habbakuk	Hab.
Zephaniah	Zeph.
Haggai	Hag.
Zechariah	Zech.
Malachi	Mal.

New Testament

Matthew	Matt.
Mark	Mark
Luke	Luke
John	John
Acts	Acts
Romans	Rom.
1 Corinthians	1 Cor.
2 Corinthians	2 Cor.
Galatians	Gal.
Ephesians	Eph.
Philippians	Phil.
Colossians	Col.
1 Thessalonians	1 Thess.
2 Thessalonians	2 Thess.
1 Timothy	1 Tim.
2 Timothy	2 Tim.
Titus	Titus
Philemon	Philem.
Hebrews	Heb.
James	James
1 Peter	1 Pet.
2 Peter	2 Pet.
1 John	1 John
2 John	2 John
3 John	3 John
Jude	Jude
Revelation	Rev.

Personal Spiritual Journal

DATE _____

_____

_____

_____

_____

_____

_____

_____

_____

_____

_____

_____

_____

My Prayer Today—

_____

_____

_____

_____

Personal Spiritual Journal

DATE _____

_____

_____

_____

_____

_____

_____

_____

_____

_____

_____

_____

_____

My Prayer Today—

_____

_____

_____

_____

Personal Spiritual Journal   DATE _____

_____

_____

_____

_____

_____

_____

_____

_____

_____

_____

_____

_____

My Prayer Today—

_____

_____

_____

_____

Personal Spiritual Journal

DATE _____

_____

_____

_____

_____

_____

_____

_____

_____

_____

_____

_____

_____

My Prayer Today—

_____

_____

_____

_____

Personal Spiritual Journal

DATE _____

_____

_____

_____

_____

_____

_____

_____

_____

_____

_____

_____

_____

_____

My Prayer Today—

_____

_____

_____

_____

Personal Spiritual Journal

DATE _____

_____

_____

_____

_____

_____

_____

_____

_____

_____

_____

_____

_____

_____

My Prayer Today—

_____

_____

_____

_____

Personal Spiritual Journal

DATE _____

_____

_____

_____

_____

_____

_____

_____

_____

_____

_____

_____

_____

My Prayer Today—

_____

_____

_____

_____

Personal Spiritual Journal

DATE _____

_____

_____

_____

_____

_____

_____

_____

_____

_____

_____

_____

_____

My Prayer Today—

_____

_____

_____

_____

Personal Spiritual Journal

DATE _____

_____

_____

_____

_____

_____

_____

_____

_____

_____

_____

_____

_____

_____

My Prayer Today—

_____

_____

_____

_____

Personal Spiritual Journal

DATE _____

_____

_____

_____

_____

_____

_____

_____

_____

_____

_____

_____

_____

_____

_____

My Prayer Today—

_____

_____

_____

_____

Personal Spiritual Journal

DATE _____

_____

_____

_____

_____

_____

_____

_____

_____

_____

_____

_____

_____

_____

My Prayer Today—

_____

_____

_____

_____

Personal Spiritual Journal

DATE _____

_____

_____

_____

_____

_____

_____

_____

_____

_____

_____

_____

_____

_____

My Prayer Today—

_____

_____

_____

_____

Personal Spiritual Journal

DATE _____

_____

_____

_____

_____

_____

_____

_____

_____

_____

_____

_____

_____

_____

My Prayer Today—

_____

_____

_____

_____

Personal Spiritual Journal

DATE _____

_____

_____

_____

_____

_____

_____

_____

_____

_____

_____

_____

_____

_____

My Prayer Today—

_____

_____

_____

_____

Personal Spiritual Journal

DATE _____

_____

_____

_____

_____

_____

_____

_____

_____

_____

_____

_____

_____

_____

_____

My Prayer Today—

_____

_____

_____

_____

Personal Spiritual Journal

DATE _____

_____

_____

_____

_____

_____

_____

_____

_____

_____

_____

_____

_____

_____

My Prayer Today—

_____

_____

_____

_____

Personal Spiritual Journal

DATE _____

_____

_____

_____

_____

_____

_____

_____

_____

_____

_____

_____

_____

My Prayer Today—

_____

_____

_____

_____

Personal Spiritual Journal

DATE _____

_____

_____

_____

_____

_____

_____

_____

_____

_____

_____

_____

_____

_____

My Prayer Today—

_____

_____

_____

_____

Personal Spiritual Journal

DATE _____

_____

_____

_____

_____

_____

_____

_____

_____

_____

_____

_____

_____

My Prayer Today—

_____

_____

_____

_____

Personal Spiritual Journal

DATE _____

_____

_____

_____

_____

_____

_____

_____

_____

_____

_____

_____

_____

My Prayer Today—

_____

_____

_____

_____